Vigilance

Vigilance

A Story of Sheriff Watson

Andrea Knies

Columbus, Ohio

Vigilance: A Story of Sheriff Watson

Published by Gatekeeper Press
2167 Stringtown Rd., Suite 109
Columbus, OH 43123-2989
www.GatekeeperPress.com

Cover art by Mimi Cirbusova

Library of Congress Control Number: 2021952007

ISBN (paperback): 9781662920226

Vigilance is a work of fiction.
Though some characters, incidents, and dialogues are based on historical record, the work as a whole is a product of the author's imagination.

Introductions

Sheriff Watson's Family

Sheriff Alexander "Sandy" Watson, b.1840
Rebecca Unity Hough Watson, b.1846 - d.1883

Clement, b.1869
Frances (Fannie), b.1874
Wade and William, b.1876
Eva, b.1878
Alexander, b.1879
Clifford, b.1883

Charles Abbe's Family

Charles Elliott Abbe, b.1831 - d.1884
Charlotte R. Scofield Abbe, b.1838

Caroline (Carrie), b.1858
Nellie, b.1861 - m.1879 Furman Whitaker

Members of the Sara Sota* Vigilance Committee Tried for Murder

Titles are their role in the Vigilance Committee.

Alfred Bidwell, Judge
Dr. Leonard Andrews, Judge
Jason Alford, Captain
Louis Cato, Lieutenant
Charles Willard, Lieutenant
Dr. Adam Hunter
Joseph Anderson
Edmond Bacon
Tom Drymond

*Although the name of the town is spelled Sarasota as one word, the historical documents record the name of the group as two words.

This is factual information reflecting their lives during the years of 1884 - 1885, which is the timeframe of this historical novel.

Chapter One

Christmas has not been the same since Rebecca passed away. Well, frankly, nothing has been. We are blessed with supportive family and friends who have helped me with the cooking and cleaning and all. But raising seven kids is a two-person job, and since that fateful day last year, I have struggled to keep the family together.

I twirl the branch of beautyberry that I brought with me between my fingers. Rebecca and I used to argue about this shrub in our yard. I found it unruly and thought that it made the homestead look messy; she loved the deep purple color of the clusters of small berries and convinced me to keep it. Now, I cherish the plant because it reminds me so much of her and her beautiful way of seeing the world. I place the sprig on her headstone and trace the engraving with my fingers, "Rebecca U. Watson, Died March 3, 1883." I bow my head for a moment of silent prayer before turning and walking away. As I leave the cemetery, I quickly wipe away the tear that has fallen to my cheek and take a deep breath. The children need me to be strong, tomorrow is Christmas after all. I hop up on the seat of my wagon, and with a quick slap of the reigns, the horses start their slow trot home.

It feels like the temperature might be almost 70 degrees today, and the skies are bright blue. The mild climate is one of the many benefits of living in Florida. Rebecca's brother John and I both fought for the Confederacy during the War between the States. When the war ended, there was nothing left for us in Mississippi; so, John went to find a place to start anew. He was the first to discover the Village of Manatee, and Rebecca and I quickly followed. Our new home is near the Gulf of Mexico about 60 miles south of old Fort Brooke, which is also called Tampa. We live along the beautiful Manatee River where the land is plentiful, and the people are the kindest I have ever known. We got our fresh start for sure, but in my wildest dreams I never thought I would be sheriff of this entire county-- all 5,000 square miles of it.

Even over the sound of the horse's hooves on the hard ground, I can hear the laughter of the children coming from inside the house. I walk up the stairs to the front porch to be greeted by the twins Will and Wade before I even make it to the door. They excitedly show me the Christmas decorations they made. They each hand me an orange with cloves stuck in neat rows. I carefully examine each one.

"You did a mighty fine job, boys!" I exclaim. I hand them each their orange back and pat their heads with approval. Both have full heads of dark hair, just like their mother's. As they run back into the house, my oldest boy Clem attempts to calm them down. But that is a fruitless task on a regular day and down near impossible on Christmas Eve. It is hard to believe that Clem is only fifteen years old. He grew up fast when his mother passed, and I now depend on him—probably more than I should.

"Papa," Fannie, my eldest daughter, calls to me from upstairs, "I need your help with something." I climb the stairs to find her frantically stuffing eight stockings as full as she can with fruit, candy, and small gifts.

"Quick, close the door," she whispers as I enter the room. "Clem and I went down to the general store and purchased all the treats for Christmas. The little ones are going to be so pleased when they see their stockings stuffed to the brim!"

I kiss Fannie on the top of her head. She has such a generous soul. She is only ten years old, but she always thinks of her younger siblings before herself.

"You were able to get all of this with the money that I gave you?" I ask with some concern.

"Well," she replies sheepishly, "Mr. Easterling did add a few items as a gift from him. I hope you aren't upset, Papa. He just wants the children to have a magical Christmas."

"No, my dear, I am not upset. You did a wonderful job, and we are bound to have a joyous day."

The sun sets early during these winter months, so it is dark by the time we sit down for supper. I light the candles on the tree to provide the perfect glow for the evening. Baby Clifford chews on his stewed potatoes while the rest of us enjoy the boiled chicken and biscuits that Fannie managed to prepare for us while doing all of the housework.

"Wonderful meal, Fannie," I say as I gulp down my last swallow of milk.

"Thank you, Papa," she replies with a blush. Clem stands and begins to clear the plates from the tables.

"The dishes can wait," I say. Clem is visibly startled; he has become accustomed to the structure and order that

I command of the family. "Tonight is a special day. Join me around the tree. I have a story to tell you." I pick a book off the shelf and begin, "'Twas the night before Christmas . . ."

By the time I finish reading the book, Will, Wade, Eva, and Alexander are fast asleep on the rug by the Christmas tree, and Clifford is sleeping soundly in Clem's arms. Clem helps me carry them one by one upstairs to their beds as Fannie cleans the dishes. Once the house is settled for the night and all the children are asleep, I blow out the candles on the tree. Tomorrow is Christmas, a day to celebrate and focus on the many blessings that we have here in Manatee County. I carefully hang our nine stockings from the mantle. Eight are stuffed full and one is empty; I just cannot make myself to leave Rebecca's in the box.

~~~~~~~

I hear the rustling of the children before I open my eyes. Their laughter is my favorite sound, so I lie there for a while just to listen to them. After a few moments, I grab my robe and slippers and creep down the stairs to view the action. Will and Wade are desperately trying to peek inside their stockings while Fannie stands sternly in front of the mantle, reminding them that it is not proper to open our stockings before Papa is awake. Little Alex and Eva stare wide-eyed at the stockings but do not dare to disobey their older sister.

"Pa's awake!" Wade exclaims the moment he catches a glimpse of me on the stairs. At the same time Will lunges at the stockings, and they all begin looking through the gifts that Fannie had so thoughtfully selected for each of her siblings.
~~~~~~~

Fannie slowly investigates her stocking and opens her mouth in shock. I had stopped by Miss Daisy's millinery and added some special ribbon in her stocking. She deserves a surprise as well.

"Oh, Papa! This is perfect," she says as she puts her arms around my neck in gratitude.

"Don't thank me," I say with a wink. "This is obviously from Father Christmas." I don't often lose track of time, but as I sit in my chair and watch the children excitedly enjoy their gifts, it slipped away from me.

I reluctantly order, "I know you are all excited about your gifts, but it is time for us to get ready for church."

The children leave their gifts and run upstairs to put on their best outfits for Christmas mass. I wear my finest suit and stop at the mirror to comb my beard and mustache before I head downstairs.

"Hurry up, the wagon will be ready in five minutes," I holler at the children as I head out the door. I walk across our yard to the stable and find Clem already harnessing our horses as I enter.

"Thank you for your help, Clem," I say as I grab the blankets from the corner of the stall. Clem nods in his typical, stoic way. He sure is like me; sometimes, I think he is too much like me. He was never one to show emotion, and since the death of his mother, he has simply thrown himself into his work.

We bring the wagon around to the front of the house. Will and Wade run through the front door, across the porch, and down the front steps as Fannie chases behind them with a comb. Her new ribbons are tied perfectly at the end of her two long braids that bounce on her back as she runs.

"Boys!" she cries with a motherly tinge in her voice, "You will not go to church looking like that!"

Clem manages to grab one under each of his arms, and Fannie does her best to tame those thick heads of hair. I chuckle as I go in the house to pick up Clifford and usher Eva and Alex out the door.

We ride into the churchyard just as the Curry family is arriving.

"Merry Christmas, John!" I yell as I wave to him and his family. His wife Elizabeth takes Clifford from my arms and smothers him with kisses. Since Rebecca's death, the Currys have become like family to us. I can't image how I would have made it through the sorrow and kept the family going if it weren't for John and Elizabeth.

"Why, Fannie," Elizabeth exclaims, "are those new ribbons in your hair? You look absolutely beautiful."

"Thank you, Mrs. Curry," Fannie responds with respect and admiration. Elizabeth has been a wonderful role model for Fannie, teaching her how to keep house and prepare meals for a large family while possessing grace.

We all walk into the small wooden church together. It wasn't much, but we had a building and a dedicated reverend, which was more than most communities in southern Florida. Many towns are still dependent on the inconsistency of a circuit rider if they are even that fortunate.

My family fills an entire pew with Will and Wade placed strategically on opposite ends to try to dampen their youthful banter.

I attempt to concentrate on the reverend's words, but my mind tends to wander back to Rebecca's funeral when I am in this place. Between fighting the war and settling a new land, I know that every person in this church has experienced loss and heartache. I try to bring myself into the present moment and be grateful for my blessings, but I just can't stop envisioning her casket at the front of the church. I cast my eyes to the ground, attempting to erase the image and join the congregation. "Joy to the world! The Lord is come," we all sing together.

After the service, the churchyard is full of heartfelt handshakes and hugs as family and neighbors wish each other a merry Christmas. The Village of Manatee is not large. We do not have the comforts of some of the big cities up north, but we are all in this together. I can depend on this community in a way that I am certain the people in the big cities would envy.

Our Christmas dinner is pure perfection. John Curry had taken Clem along on their hunting trip last week. Clem returned beaming with pride and, thankfully, with a turkey. Elizabeth helped Fannie prepare the large bird and now we all sit around the table with a beautiful feast before us. We join hands in prayer and gratitude.

"Dear Lord," I begin, "we thank you for this bountiful meal. And for the wonderful work of Clement and Frances who prepared this meal for our family. And we thank you for our kind neighbors, the roof over our heads, this prosperous year, and the health of our family. Please continue to bless and protect us during the upcoming year. And finally, dear Lord, please tell Rebecca that we love her and miss her."

"Amen," the family says in unison.

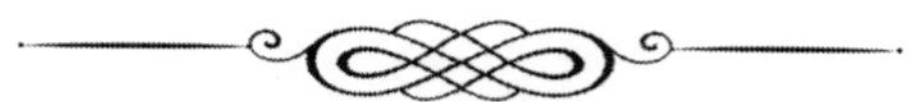

Chapter Two

It is a couple of days after Christmas, just after sundown, when I hear the thunderous approach of a horse. I look out the front window and see one of the Whitaker boys jumping down from the saddle.

"Clem, isn't that Emile Whitaker, Bill's youngest?" I ask.

"Sure is, Pa," he replies as he joins me at the window. "I wonder what could possibly bring him all the way out here this time of the night."

My palms begin to sweat. I know that there is no good reason for him to make this trip from Sarasota alone. Something terrible must have occurred. Emile barely had time to hitch his horse when I hear him pounding on the door.

"Sheriff Watson, Sheriff Watson," he says between gasping breaths. I ask Fannie to bring him a glass of water. He drinks it swiftly and then looks at me with terrified eyes and says, "Mister Abbe has been murdered."

"Clem, take Emile out to the porch. This is not a conversation for the young ones to hear." I then turn to Fannie. "I need you to keep the children in the house," I say sternly.

I walk out onto the porch and close the door tightly behind me. The night is so quiet that I swear I can hear the river rushing nearby. The moon lights up the two boys as they whisper in the corner. Emile props himself against the porch railing for support. Clem and Emile are right around the same age and are usually doing whatever they can to look tough but not tonight. As I walk over to them, I hear the tremble in their voices.

"Pa," Clem whispers, "it's really bad."

"Sheriff Watson," Emile's voice quakes as he speaks. I place a hand on the boy's shoulder.

"Call me Sandy, son," I say as I attempt to calm his shattered nerves. "Take a deep breath and tell me what you know."

"Charlie Willard shot Mr. Abbe this afternoon," he said in a low reverent tone. His voice steadies as he continues to share the grim news. "It was in the middle of the afternoon, Sheriff Sandy, in the middle of the street."

"Now why would Charlie want to kill the postmaster?" I wonder aloud.

"I don't rightly know, but everyone is struck with fear. Mrs. Abbe is at my house now."

"I am going to gather my hat and pistol, and I will ride back to Sarasota with you."

"I am going with you, Pa," Clem states with confidence. "You will need help."

"I appreciate your offer, son, but I need you here with the family. I will not be back home tonight, and I will send word if it's going to be longer than that. However, you are correct, I should not go alone. I will stop by John Curry's house on the way and see if one of his sons will accompany us."

I take Clem by the shoulders and look him directly in the eyes. "Listen, I don't know what's happening, but I have a terrible feeling about it. So, keep the kids in the house until you hear from me and keep the shotgun close to you at all times, you hear." Clem nods, the gravity of the situation was clear to us all.

"Now, Clem, harness our horses and Emile's horse to the wagon. I don't want Emile riding any more tonight." He nods and he and Emile head to the barn.

Wade, Will, and Fannie rush to my side as I enter the house. Fannie had put the youngest to bed while I was out on the porch.

"I need to go to Sarasota tonight, children." I muster a small smile as I hug them all tightly. They look up at me with terrified faces. "Boys, I need two lanterns for the wagon and my canteen." The twins rush to gather my requests as I fasten my holster and slide my pistol to its comfortable spot on my hip.

Fannie watches me with concern; she is not fooled by my false smile.

"Papa," her eyes glisten as she holds back tears, "please be safe." I pin my badge to my jacket, grab my hat from the hook by the door, and give her one more tight hug.

~~~~~~~

The first stop Emile and I make is at the Curry homestead. John is understandably surprised when I knock on his door.

"Sandy, what's the matter?" he asks, too concerned to bother with proper pleasantries. He walks out of the house and joins me on the porch. I notice his wife Elizabeth watching from the window.

"John, I have a favor to ask of you. There has been a murder in Sarasota."

"Who was it?" John lowers his voice as to not create alarm with his family.

"Charles Abbe," I state as a matter of fact. "I was hoping your oldest Arvid would be willing to accompany Emile Whitaker and me on the journey. You know I would never ask if it wasn't dire."

"The postmaster!" he exclaims. "I know people aren't a fan of his politics, but I didn't think those bastards would take it this far."

"According to Emile it was Charlie Willard, but you understand why I can't wait until morning to begin the investigation."
~~~~~~~

"Arvid!" John shouts into the house, "Please join the Sheriff and me outside." Arvid is a strong twenty-year-old young man. He stands as tall as I do and slightly taller than his father.

"I'm sorry to come to you at this time of night, Arvid, but I am in desperate need of assistance." I explain the situation, and he agrees to accompany us without hesitation.

As John and I wait for Arvid to gather his gun and inform his mother about the unexpected trip, I have one more favor to ask of John.

"I know I have asked so much of you and Elizabeth over the past couple of years and I appreciate everything you have done for us. I hate to keep burdening you, but will you please check on the children in the morning, and," I take a deep breath, "I don't know what I'm dealing with, and if I . . . if I don't return, John, will you please take care of my children?"

"There is no need to talk like that, Sandy. Everything is going to be fine," he states with shaken confidence. "But for your peace of mind, of course, it would be our honor. You know we love your children as if they were our own."

Arvid comes out to the porch, followed by his mother. She hands me a basket of bread and fruit.

"You will need your energy," she says. "The children and I will pray tonight. We will pray that you, Arvid, and Emile have a safe journey. We will pray for Mrs. Abbe and her children, and we will pray that the murderer is brought to justice."

"Elizabeth, we all appreciate your kindness." I take the basket, then Arvid and I join Emile in the wagon. Emile smiles as I hand him the basket of food from Elizabeth, and I soon smell the sweetness of an orange as he hungrily eats.

We start the journey to Sarasota. During the day it could easily take a few hours; the road is sandy and full of roots and washouts. But traveling in the darkness adds more challenges, mainly panthers, bears, and bobcats. Thank goodness the alligators are usually quiet at night. To conserve oil, we only light one of the lanterns. The brightness of the moon continues to prove a blessing as we slowly ride over the bumpy ground. Despite the jostling of the wagon on the bumpy path, I look back to see that Emile has fallen fast asleep.

About an hour into the trip, Arvid finally gathers the courage to ask, "Sheriff Watson, what should I expect when we arrive in Sarasota?"

"Well, I suppose we will begin at the Whitaker homestead so we can talk to Mrs. Abbe. Then we'll have to explore the location where the murder took place to gather evidence."

"Yes, Sir," he responds respectfully. "The investigation process seems clear, but will we be safe? I have never known anyone who has been murdered before."

I think carefully before responding; this is new territory for me as well. You don't receive training when you take on the role of sheriff on the frontier. Sheriff Hayman, who held the post prior to my election, was a wonderful mentor. He spent many hours providing me with the skills and knowledge I needed, and of course, fighting in the war honed my marksmanship and strategic abilities. But there are some things that you just can't prepare for. People have been killed during my time as sheriff, but this is different. I have heard stories about tensions building in Sarasota between some of the members of the community, but I never thought it would end in a cold-blooded murder.

"I understand your concerns, and honestly, I do not know what to expect. But I'll keep you out of harm's way." I open my mouth to add "I promise" but stop. I honor my word, and do not make promises that I am not sure I will be able to keep. We stop speaking at this point, both lost in our own thoughts. The sound of the wagon wheels keeps us company, and the occasional rustle of an animal in the brush breaks the silence.

We manage to make it to the Whitaker's homestead Yellow Bluffs by midnight. Even at that late hour, the house is aglow with light. It feels like a beacon after the long dark journey. As we pull up to the house, Mary Whitaker rushes out of the door to embrace Emile. Under normal circumstances, I am sure this would have embarrassed the boy, but tonight he simply places his head on her shoulder and welcomes the comfort. Mary's husband Bill follows close behind.

"Well done, boy," Bill praises his son for his bravery and the success on his mission. Mary invites us all inside, and I soon see that the house is packed with people.

In addition to Bill, Mary, and all their children, Charlotte Abbe is there with her daughter Nellie. Nellie had recently married Bill and Mary's son Furman. Charlotte is pacing around the room wringing her hands in panic.

Sitting in a chair at the end of the table is the young man who has been boarding at the Abbe's house, Charles Moorehouse. His elbows are on the table with his forehead cradled in his hands and his eyes are closed. However, the sad shaking of his head indicates that he is not at rest, simply deep in thought.

There are also several other people from the community in the house that have gathered to show support and assist in this terrible time.

They all look up when I enter the house; the room falls silent. I look around at their faces for a moment, the fireplace pops, and one of Bill's sons goes over to add a log to the flame. I walk slowly over to the widow.

"Mrs. Abbe, you have my deepest sympathy. I am so sorry for your loss." I attempt to maintain my professional demeanor, but when the poor woman begins to tremble, I forget about all of that and put an arm around her shoulders.

"Lotta," I say in a hushed tone, "I promise I will bring whoever did this to justice." And that was a promise I intend to keep. "Charlotte, do you mind if we go out to the porch to talk?"

"I would rather not, Sheriff," she replies. "I would prefer to stay in the house if possible. He is still out there." It is clear that she is in a deep state of shock and fear.

"Ma," her daughter Nellie says, "we will just step right outside the door, and if it's all right with the sheriff, I'll go with you."

"That's fine with me, Mrs. Whitaker," I reply to Nellie. "Will that be satisfactory for you, Mrs. Abbe?" She nods and walks with Nellie and me to the porch. Once outside, she takes a deep breath and looks up at the bright moon.

"I just can't believe it," she says, "I can't believe that someone killed Charles. I know that people are envious of his success; I know they disagreed with his politics . . . but murder? I didn't think this would ever happen."

"My thoughts precisely," I reply. "I understand that this is terribly unsettling to discuss, but I need to know what happened today." She nods and I wait for her to begin. Nellie patiently holds her mother's hand.

"Charles and our boarder Charles Moorehouse had been working on this old boat down by the bay all morning. They came in around noon for dinner. I'd say it was about half past one when they left the house again to head back down to the bay. That was the last time I saw him." She pauses and I wait while she wipes away her tears with her handkerchief.

"It was only about half an hour later when I heard the gun shots. It was obviously Leonard Andrews's shotgun because his gun malfunctions, making the first shot set off the second. It's distinct and everyone knows the sound." She pauses once more. I was surprised that she said it was Andrews's gun. Emile was sure that Charlie Willard killed Abbe. I don't interrupt. It is important that I let her tell the story. As I wait, we hear the large group in the house, but the porch and the moon provide a place of peace.

"When I saw Charles Moorehouse running towards the house, I just knew. 'Did they kill my husband?' I screamed at him as I ran in the direction of the shots. He begged me to stay away. Said they would kill me too, but I was not in my right mind. I kept running to find my husband." She tries to continue but is not finding the words.

"It's ok, Ma," Nellie says calmly as she pats the back of her mother's hand. "Take your time." Several minutes pass before Mrs. Abbe is able continue.

"Like I was saying," she begins, "I kept running until I saw the blood, his hat, the paint cans that he had been carrying. But Charles was not there, there was no body. I pounded on the door to Alfred Bidwell's store to find someone to help. I screamed and screamed, but no one responded. I tried to open the door, but it was locked." She looks up to the moon again.

That's another odd piece of information. Why would Bidwell close his store on a Saturday afternoon, one of the busiest times for trade?

"I began to run to the bay. Honestly, Sheriff, my memory gets a bit faint at this point."

"That's understandable, after what you just experienced. All I ask is that you do your best. You have been incredibly helpful thus far," I reassure her.

"Well, from what I can recall, I ran to the bay. Mr. Cunliff was on his wharf and saw me in a panic. He came to me and tried to calm me down. Then he walked me back to my home."

I assume she is finished, but then she remembers one more piece of information.

"The Hunters, they live by the store. They were there when it happened. They saw me screaming. I don't know why they didn't help me."

This is clearly all the poor woman can recall at the moment. Nellie walks with her mother back into the house. There are already many inconsistencies and questions. I sit down on the porch steps to get a moment to regain my senses, but I am not going to get a break. I hear footsteps behind me, and then George Riggin takes a seat on the step. George is well respected in this area and lives near me by the river in the Village of Manatee. As he is a bright young man, I am grateful that he is the one that sat next to me. At least it is someone with whom I can discuss the current state of this investigation.

"Sheriff Watson," he begins, "I want you to know that I am here to assist you. This murderer cannot be left to run free. I fear that the entire community will become a lawless place of corruption if we do not bring him to justice."

"I completely agree, George. And I am mighty obliged to your offer to assist. We all know that this is going to be long, difficult, and dangerous." We sit for another moment.

"Please bring Charles Moorehouse out to me." George and I both rise from our spots on the steps, and he enters the house to fetch Mr. Moorehouse.

Charles Moorehouse has been visiting from Chicago and boarding with the Abbe family. He is acquainted with their daughter Carrie, who is also in Chicago, where she teaches school. He is about twenty years of age, tall, slim, and obviously rattled by the events of the day. I believe it is safe to assume that this situation is not what he anticipated when he decided to visit Florida.

I introduce myself to the young man as he steps out on to the porch and ask him to tell me what happened today.

"I understand the importance of what I have to tell you," he replies, "but, Sheriff, you didn't see the look in the eyes of those men. I am frightened for my life, for all of our lives."

"I am terribly sorry that you find yourself in this situation, Mr. Moorehouse, but as the only eyewitness, you are the key to unraveling this murder." As Moorehouse looks up at the moon, I notice that many people are finding solace in the moon tonight. I believe that people look to something dependable in times like these, and the moon is about as steadfast a thing as one can find.

Charles slowly begins, "We were working on the boat that morning, minding our own business, when two men approached us from the south. They were introduced to me as Fred Jones and Charlie Willard. Out of nowhere, Willard started talking about politics and got more and more heated as he spoke. He mentioned that he is proud to fly his President Cleveland flag and asked me if I was a republican like Mr. Abbe. When I replied that I was, his voice got louder as he spewed many vulgarities against the party." Charles stops for a moment to gather his thoughts.

"Mr. Abbe and I returned to the house to eat around noon. While we were eating, Mr. Abbe decided that we didn't need to work anymore today so we headed to the boat to gather our tools. I pushed the wheelbarrow." His voice begins to crack a bit as he continues with the story.

"By about two o'clock, we had gathered what we needed and were headed back to the house. Then I spotted a couple of men sitting on a pile of lumber outside of Bidwell's store. I only recognized one of them. It was Willard. I will never forget his angry face. Then he aimed that gun and shot poor Mr. Abbe in the head. He dropped straight to the ground, and I bent down trying to help him, but then Willard yelled at me to run for my life." He begins to speak quickly as if he wants to finish reliving this event as fast as he can.

"So, I ran. I only looked back once as I was running, and I saw Willard dragging Mr. Abbe's body towards the store. At that point, they were out of my view, and I ran to Charlotte to let her know what happened. I tried to stop her from running to the scene, but she was in quite a state, and she ignored my pleas." He stops abruptly, and when he speaks again, it was calm and clear.

"That's all I know, Sheriff, may I please go back inside the house?"

"Yes, thank you. You were extremely helpful," I reply. "Will you please ask George Riggin to join me out here?" He nods with relief and heads back in the house.

"You need me, Sheriff?" George says as he steps out of the door.

"Yes, George. Let's gather a few men and head to the scene." I instruct. "We can't waste any time in this investigation."

George returns with Arvid and two other men from the community. We mount our horses and head south towards the scene. The bright, dependable moon leads our way.

Chapter Three

The five of us leave the chaos of Yellow Bluffs and are soon engulfed in the silence of the night. We ride south for a bit until we pass the Abbe's home and then turn westward towards the bay and Bidwell's store-- the same route Charles Abbe walked just twelve hours earlier.

I am not sure if there will be anything left at the scene, but even in the dark we easily find the large puddle of blood in the middle of the sandy road. I notice as the other men look up to the stars and release silent prayers to the sky.

George is the first to speak, "They didn't even bother to cover their tracks, Sheriff. It's almost like they wanted to get caught."

"Or they didn't think it would be investigated," I hear one of the riders retort from behind me. I ignore the comment and dismount my horse; my hand is on my pistol as I hit the ground.

"Everyone be prepared and alert," I warn. "We do not know if the murderer is still around."

The blood on the ground covers an area approximately one foot in diameter. That's much more blood than an average gunshot wound would create. I suspect that the murderer also slit poor Abbe's throat.

"George, please inspect that item," I say as I point towards a white object a few feet closer to the bay. George picks up what is left of a white straw hat.

"What's this?" he questions as he picks something out of the hat. Even in the darkness, I can see his face turn pale at the realization of what he has in his hand. There were many things I saw while fighting in the war, and I instantly recognize the brain tissue that George drops back into the hat.

I move closer to George and the hat in his hand to examine the evidence. There are short gray hairs stuck to the brain matter, Charles Abbe's short gray hairs.

"Wrap that in your bandana and put it in my saddle bag," I instruct as I bend to get a better look at the trail of blood. Without a word, I begin to follow the trail while the others follow closely behind me.

As we approach the bay, we see something glistening on top of one of the bright white sand dunes. It's a good quality .44-caliber pistol. I pick it up and can't help but hear the words stated earlier begin to echo in my ear. Maybe they truly didn't believe that I would seriously investigate this crime. I pick up the pistol and walk to the end of the wharf alone.

Those homesteading in Florida live by their own set of rules. I admit there have been times that I have allowed those in the community to govern each other the best way they see fit. But as I stand here in the moonlight by the bay, I realize that we are at a crossroads. Either I bring this person to justice, or we risk Manatee County becoming a lawless land. And there are way too many people that I care about here to let that happen. I return to the shore with a newfound purpose.

"Gentlemen, we will not be able to conduct this investigation properly in the dark. We all need to get some rest; I will resume my investigation at daybreak."

George, Arvid, and I decide to sleep nearby at the Abbes' empty house. Although most of the other men return to their neighboring homes, one fellow requests to stay with us that evening. Richard Cunliff is a man in his sixties who has lived in Sarasota for ten to twelve years, which is longer than most of the locals. I anticipate that he will be an asset to this investigation. Not only does he know the land well, but also, more importantly, he knows the people.

The Abbes' house is dark and quiet, quite a stark difference from the bright, loud activity at Yellow Bluffs. The house is empty, but I can feel Charles Abbe everywhere. His good hat is still on its peg at the door, and his wooden chair at the end of the table awaits his return. We all choose to sleep on the floor in the main room because none of us want to upset the memory of the house.

Even in my exhaustion, I am not able to close my eyes. I stare up at the ceiling in the darkness. The clues are not making sense. Why did Willard kill Abbe? Was it truly just for political reasons? And why did he use Andrews's shotgun, a gun that was known by its sound? And why did they spare Charles Moorehouse? They let the eyewitness run free, and more than that, they encouraged him to run. And why did Bidwell have his store closed on a Saturday? He is known for his relentless pursuit of a dollar. I just can't shake the feeling that I am dealing with much more than a simple murder.

~~~~~~~

When the morning sun wakes me, I realize that, despite the thoughts running through my mind, I must have fallen asleep. George, Arvid, and Richard are still sleeping, so I step out to the porch to stretch my weary body. I always enjoy the golden glow of a winter sunrise in Florida, but this particular morning I am more grateful than ever for the warmth and light. I hear rustling in the house, but I stay on the porch for a few more moments. I know that I must continue my work, but I am not looking forward to the day that stands before me. When I finally join the others inside, I see the exhaustion in their eyes and imagine that I must look the same.

We leave the house and take the short journey back to the murder scene. The large bloodstain is still obvious on the ground and, with the light of day, the trail that leads from it is much easier to follow. I spot some prints in the sand that were not visible during the night.

"George, Arvid, please grab some of those boards," I instruct as I point to a pile near a wharf. They quickly attend to the task without asking any questions. "Place them on either side of these shoe marks." It is not easy to preserve evidence in the sand, so we need to gather as much information from the clues as we are able.

"George, what size shoe do you wear?" I ask.
~~~~~~~

"A number eight," he replies. We line his foot along one of the tracks and estimate that one set of footprints is a number eight like George and the other is smaller, probably a number six. As the tracks meet the water's edge, we see barefoot marks that come in from the water, meet the trail, and turn back into the bay.

"I know that foot," George states with a mixture of shock and confidence. "That is the track of Ed Bacon, one of the oysterman's sons. He never wears his shoes on the boat. The narrow width and the protruding bone by the large toe, I have seen that distinct foot many times."

Cunliff had stepped back from the scene to leave us to our work, but at the sound of Bacon's name he moves forward.

"Sheriff," he says, "I think it's time for me to tell you what I saw."

I tell Arvid and George to continue their search and walk up the slight slope from the shore to the road. From this point, we have a perfect view of the bayfront and the wharfs. The sun is at our backs and glistens on the still water. It is hard to imagine this place of beauty being the scene to such a devilish crime.

Cunliff immediately begins to talk, "I had agreed to help Jason Alford with some work on Saturday. I met up with him at Bidwell's store in the morning. There was a group of men there, and they were already drunk. They offered me a drink from their still, but I refused—I don't touch the stuff. Anyway, Jason and I finished the fence we were mending and then we all headed home around noon to eat. At that time, I saw Ed Bacon, Joe Anderson, and Adam Hunter walking up from their moonshine still at the bay. Hunter was so inebriated that he needed to be held up between the others."

Well, I think to myself, that rules out Adam Hunter. If he were that intoxicated, he would not have been able to commit the crime. I cross him off my mental list of suspects.

Cunliff continues, "After eating, I returned to Alford's home to help him with some hoeing in his tomato garden. I heard the shots, but I thought nothing of it at first. It's not an uncommon sound in these parts. Then I saw some commotion, so I stopped my work and walked to the main road."

I nod at Cunliff and continue to listen closely.

"Down at Bidwell's wharf I saw Ed Bacon's boat. I know that boat well by its green cabin. There were three men on the boat, and Joe Anderson was standing on the wharf. Later I saw the boat heading out to the pass with another small boat in tow."

And now I have a witness who can verify that Ed Bacon was indeed at the bay at that time. Coupled with his odd footprints, I have a good case against him.

"Please continue," I say to Richard. He had kindly paused when he realized that I was deep in thought.

"Then I saw poor Mrs. Abbe running around by the bay in a complete panic. I went to help her, and that's when I learned about the murder. I tried to calm her down and walk her back to her house," Richard then sighs deeply. "I had no idea what they were up to on that boat. I just can't escape the image of Mr. Abbe's body being carelessly thrown into the bay. I have never been a witness to anything so cold-blooded."

I remove my hat and wipe some sweat off my forehead. George and Arvid are still walking along the water with their heads down looking for evidence. I see some items in George's hands and hope that they have found more items to help with the investigation.

I thank Richard for his assistance, and he leaves to return to his house. Satisfied with the information we had gathered this morning, George, Arvid, and I head back to Yellow Bluffs.

~~~~~~~

We are immediately greeted by the smell of ham and fresh biscuits as we enter the house. My stomach rumbles, and I realize that I have not eaten properly since my supper at home last night. Mary ushers us to seats at the table and places a full plate in front of each of us. One of her daughters brings the water pitcher to fill our glasses, and we all express genuine gratitude.

Bill sits at the head of the table with his back to the fireplace. His calm genial manner is exactly what Charlotte Abbe needs right now. To be honest, it's exactly what I need right now as well. The table and benches where we sit were crafted by Bill and add to the comfort of his home. I relish this moment as we all devour the hearty food.

Charlotte is seated to Bill's right. I am surprised to see that she is already dressed in partial mourning attire.
~~~~~~~

Someone must have gone to her home to fetch a few things for her while we were investigating the scene this morning.

"Well," Bill begins, "what did you find?" Charlotte looks at us with exhausted blank eyes. We tell them about the white straw hat, the pistol, and the shoe marks. Charlotte recognizes the pistol and hat as Charles's. Bill is just as surprised as I am that the murderer and his accomplices were so brazen as to leave behind strong evidence. For Richard's safety, I don't share his story with the group.

A loud noise interrupts our conversation, and I look at the window to see a couple of wagons approaching the house. As they get closer, I can see that it is a group that has come down from Manatee and Braidentown. Charles Abbe didn't have a lot of friends in the Sarasota area, but he had amassed quite a few up by the river. I suspect that this group is planning to take care of the law themselves.

"Good day," I say as I walk up to the group, seven men in total.

"It was Willard," one of the men says as he hops off his buckboard. "We all know it. Why haven't you arrested him yet?" I recognized the man as Pliny, one of the Reasoner brothers who runs the nursery. Pliny is in his early twenties, I believe. I haven't interacted with him too much, but in his short time in the area he has gained the respect of many. I believe him to be a reasonable man of honor, but he has had a long journey to stir up his anger, and I am concerned that this entire group is in a state to do something regrettable.

"I am unable to answer your questions at this moment. We are in the middle of a murder investigation." I know that these men mean well, so I try to appeal to their desire for justice, "It is imperative that I conduct this investigation to the letter of the law. If this case is compromised the guilty might run free."

Pliny walks up to me, looks me square in the eyes and says, "Do you really care if the guilty run free?"

I am exhausted and my first reaction is to put this young man in his place, but instead I pause to gather my thoughts. Pliny takes that moment as an invitation to continue speaking. By this point, most of the occupants of the Whitaker home are on the porch, and the other six men from the river are all standing behind Pliny.

"You know that these men are devils, Sheriff Watson, and yet you have done nothing." Pliny is standing taller and talking slower than when he first arrived. He is gaining his composure and I decide that letting him speak might be my best course of action. "They have terrified this poor family, and for what? Because they are cowards, that's why! And you let them continue and now poor Mr. Abbe is dead!"

He stomps his right boot on the ground and the crowd behind him erupts in support of his rant. I take a deep breath and wait for them to calm.

"I am a human, Pliny. I do the best I can, but I have made mistakes. This is a tragedy, and we need to all work together to handle this case properly," I say as calmly as I am able. I like the young man, I really do, but in this moment, I want to whack him upside the head.

I don't know if I truly got through to him or not, but at least he relaxes. The group expresses their condolences to Charlotte and her family and move on, no doubt to conduct their own investigation. I hope that they don't do anything to disrupt our work, but I can't worry myself with them. I have a job to do.

The time has come to head back to the river with Arvid, and George has agreed to ride alongside of us. I thank the Whitakers for their hospitality. George mounts his horse, and Arvid and I sit in the wagon. My mind continues to process all the information that I have received, and I wish to discuss it with George, but I refrain. It is best that I wait and discuss things with Major Alden Adams, the Manatee County Justice of the Peace.

~~~~~~~~

Elizabeth Curry is at our home checking on the children when I arrive in the evening. They all run out the door to greet me and for a moment I can forget the events of last night. Even my exhaustion is temporarily alleviated as I welcome the children into my arms. Without a word, Clem takes the horses and wagon to the barn. Fannie questions when I ate last and shows me the rolls that Elizabeth just taught her to bake. Although I did fill my stomach at the Whitaker's, that was hours ago, and I am happy to try one of her fresh hot rolls.
~~~~~~~~

I thank Elizabeth for all her help, and she eagerly leaves the house to go see Arvid, who I had dropped off at the Curry place. The children and I sit around the table, and I listen intently as they tell me about everything they did while I was away. They are used to me not wanting to talk about my work while at home, and despite the curiosity of the older ones, they refrain from asking questions about my night.

It's Fannie who notices how heavy my eyes are and insists that I go upstairs to bed. She also informs me that I must leave my clothing outside of my door and she will wash it. Apparently, my children think I smell terrible.

I close the door to my room and lie down on my bed. The sun has already set on another short December day, and I drift off to sleep with a heart full of gratitude and a mind full of dread.

Chapter Four

First thing Monday morning, I head out to the homestead of Major Adams. Calling it a homestead does not do it justice. Alden Adams built himself an honest-to-goodness castle here on the Manatee River that he and his wife Adelaide refer to as Villa Zanza. It took many years to complete, and as I ride up to the home this morning, I notice that construction and planting are still taking place. That will likely be a constant occurrence with a place of this size.

I walk down a lush pathway of exotic trees and shrubs to the concrete stairs that lead to the front door. The door knocker is heavy and two loud thuds echo through the house as I strike the large wooden door. Instantly, dogs begin to howl from inside the house, and I notice the sound of another animal that I am not able to distinguish. In addition to the unusual home and the lush grounds, Major Adams and his wife keep a menagerie of animals on the grounds.

One of the servants answers the door. "Welcome, Sheriff Watson," he states formally. There is no need for introduction. The servants of this home are well acquainted with me. "Please come in. I will alert Major Adams of your arrival."

I stand and look around the opulent entryway. No matter how many times I am here, there is always something that strikes me that I have never noticed before.

Alden appears in the hallway. "Sandy, is it true?" he questions me as he shakes my hand and leads me into the house.

"I'm afraid so. Mr. Charles Abbe was murdered on Saturday in Sarasota," I reply, not anxious to recount all the details. He leads me to the room that faces north, overlooking the river. Another servant brings two glasses of tea and places the tray on the small round table between our two chairs.

I begin telling him what I have learned over my time in Sarasota. As I near the end of my findings, Adelaide walks into the room. She is an intelligent, well-traveled woman who always carries herself with grace and dignity.

"Hello, Sheriff Watson. I wish we were seeing you under better circumstances," she says.

"Good morning, Mrs. Adams," I reply as I take her hand to kiss the back of it. Adelaide wears a fine dress that could not possibly have been purchased locally. My guess is that she bought it in either Boston or Paris since they travel to both frequently. She begins speaking to Alden in, what I believe, is French to which he quickly responds. They are both multilingual and Alden claims that he speaks seven languages—although only five fluently.

Major Adams turns to me and switches seamlessly back to English, "It seems as if we have visitors, Sheriff." At that moment the servant who had greeted me at the door enters the room followed by twenty or so angry townsfolk. It is clear by the servant's mannerisms that he did not invite the group to follow him. Major Adams is a well-respected officer from the Union Army and as the men walk into the room, I see his demeanor shift. He changes from being my colleague to talking charge.

His back straightens and he bellows in a clear and direct voice, "This is not a discussion to be had in my home, gentlemen. Please take this to the Justice of the Peace office, and Sheriff Watson and I will meet you there." I both respect and envy his ability to command a crowd.

That is all it takes. The crowd leaves the house, mounts their horses, and rides to the office. Once they were gone, Major Adams looks at me, "Are you ready for this, Sandy?"

"I don't have a choice, do I?" Alden pats my back, and we leave to meet the group at his downtown office.

~~~~~~~

The angry members of the community are waiting for us outside the office door when we arrive. Alden has an office in the back of his large commissary on the main street that runs through the Village of Manatee, just south of the river. Because it is Major Adam's space, it has the finest furnishings in the area.

Alden walks through the crowd with his back stiff and his head held high. He opens the door to the commissary and the people follow him through the large storeroom. His boots make sharp sounds on the planks of the floor as he walks to the wooden door in the back that leads to his office.
~~~~~~~

His office is large with windows facing south and west. His grand, wooden desk is situated so he can easily gaze towards the west. He sits at his chair and motions for me to join him behind the desk. I stand next to him and survey the faces of the men who have followed us into the room. I recognize them all, although some I know much better than others. George Riggin gives me an encouraging nod of his head as I catch his eye, and John Curry works his way through the crowd to stand near me in quiet solidarity.

Major Adams continues to command the room of outraged men and calmly begins the process of drafting the deposition and issuing arrest warrants. In the end, all the men in the room sign the deposition and we have six warrants. It is clear that Major Adams and I will not be able to accomplish the task of gathering statements and making all of these arrests on our own. I need to gather some help.

I step forward to address the room, "I need a posse of strong, able-bodied men who are willing to ride with Major Adams and me to Sarasota to make arrests and gather the official statements. This is going to be tedious, and it is unlikely that we will return home tonight."

The first person to step forward is Pliny Reasoner. "I volunteer," he states firmly, "and I promise to uphold the letter of the law." I meet his eyes, and he nods in respect. I guess what I said to him in Sarasota resonated after all.

After Pliny volunteers, man after man steps up to assist—a true testament to the honor of our community. We agree to leave in one hour to allow those who are going to join us time to return to their homes and gather their guns and supplies.

This also gives me time to, once again, tell my children that it is unlikely that I will return home tonight.

~~~~~~~

As Major Adams and I begin the journey, we are accompanied by twenty-four other men, all armed, some on horses, and others riding in the wagons that we will need to bring the suspects back to await the trial.

We ride quickly and, upon arrival, immediately begin taking the statements from anyone in the neighborhood that has information. Although we had brought several sheets of paper with us, we soon find that we must use any piece of paper we can find to take the multitude of statements. Many members of the community share accounts of threats and malicious behavior directed toward Charles Abbe.

It had rained a little overnight, causing the air to be full of humidity and mosquitoes. I walk over to the side of the road to take shelter under a stately live oak tree. I remove my hat to fan my face and provide some relief from both the heat and the bugs. I notice that the post office is open. I walk across the street to find Charlotte Abbe behind the counter.

"You look surprised, Sheriff." She stands tall behind the counter in her deep mourning attire. The full black dress is made of simple cotton without any trim, but has the customary high collar, cuffs, and shawl. Her weeping veil is short, ending just past her shoulders and made of black crepe
~~~~~~~

attached to a small silk bonnet. The garments are not as nice as she would have had when they lived in St. Louis, but she still stood tall with dignity and respect. I wonder momentarily if she is going to have a brooch made with her husband's hair, but quickly remember that, unless I find the body, neither a memento nor a wake would be possible.

"Did you really think I would let these thugs prevent the post office from opening?" She rouses me from my thoughts.

I admire her courage and sense of duty. When Rebecca passed, I also threw myself back into my work to provide some routine in the middle of the chaos and to momentarily escape the sorrow.

"No, Mrs. Abbe, your character has never been in doubt." Throughout the entire conversation, she continues to stand tall, but I occasionally hear her voice crack with sorrow and fear. At the end of our conversation, I tip my hat at the brave woman and leave to rejoin the posse.

I stand at the crest of the road just before it begins its descent to the water. It is hard to describe the way I feel. Even amid twenty-five armed men, I feel paranoid. Charles Willard is still at-large, and until we have him behind bars, I will not be able to shake the feeling that someone is watching me.

Throughout the day's questioning, we learn that it is believed that Willard is still residing at Chandler Yonge's homestead a little further south by Phillippi Creek. Although the posse worked all day without taking breaks, we have one more stop to make. It was near midnight when we finally arrive at Yonge's homestead. I instruct the group to tie their horses away from the house so that they do not hear us approaching.

We walk slowly; the house is dark. We are close when a dog barks loudly. He must have alerted the members of the house because the next thing we see is a figure running from the house toward the creek.

Some members of the posse take off after him on foot, and shots are fired. Some run back to fetch their horses. While the posse continues the search, I see Chandler standing on his porch with a shotgun in hand.

"Do you have a warrant?" he bellows at me as I approach.

"Yes," I say loudly, as I hold up the warrant with my left hand for him to see. My right hand is tightly wrapped around the handle of my pistol. "We have a warrant for the arrest of Charles Willard for the murder of Charles Abbe and have been informed that he stays here with you. Is that correct?" I stand my ground and continue up the stairs to look him in the eyes.

"Yeah, that's right, he stays here," he flashes a devilish grin, "but he's not here now." I knew that was true, but I insist on searching the home just in case. I motion for George to join me.

We find some daily items such as his hat and cigarette papers on his bureau, but nothing of significance. Alden is waiting for us when we exit the house.

"We haven't been able to find him, Sheriff. Any luck in the house?" I tell him about our findings, and we agree to call off the posse for the night.

As much as I hate to give Willard the night to escape, it is clear that he isn't running to anywhere in particular, he is just running scared. The wilderness of Florida does not take kindly to solitary humans. He won't be able to last for long. We simply need to chase him until he is unable to go any further.

Earlier in the day, Cunliff had kindly offered his land for us to set up camp for the night. Now, we all lie on the ground and look up at the stars, but with Willard on the run and Abbe's body still missing, none of us can relax.

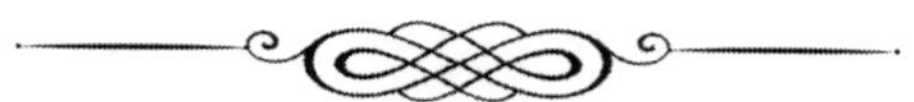

Chapter Five

Tuesday morning's sunrise brings a hazy pink hue. The posse slowly begins to move again. They are all groggy from a short and restless sleep but do seem to appreciate the light of day. As they begin to eat some of the food that we had packed with us, Major Adams and I plan our day's strategy. Alden and I will start the day by gathering more formal testimonies for the official court record and dividing the others in the posse into groups to continue the search for Willard. This afternoon, we will begin looking for the body.

I stand in front of the men and split them into groups; we have no time to waste.

"You," I say as I point one by one at eight men, "take your horses and search the area around the Yonge homestead. You," I point at another ten, "go looking on foot." I address the entire gathering, "And never stray on your own. Always be with at least one other man. We know what Willard is capable of, and he has more people on his side." Those men fill their canteens at Cunliff's well and prepare the search. I instruct the remaining six men to come with Major Adams and me to collect more testimonies.

The men searching for Willard head south, and Major Adams and our men return to the Abbes' house. It is still early, and Charlotte has not yet left to tend to the post office. She sits at the table with her daughter Nellie, son-in-law Furman, and Charles Moorehouse, enjoying some breakfast.

At the sight of us, she immediately offers food to our group. I politely decline and inform her that we all ate a little this morning.

"How are you this morning, Mrs. Abbe?"

She straightens in her chair, and it appears that she might have finally had a full night's sleep.

"We are sending word to Carrie in Chicago about the death of her father," she replies. Their youngest daughter Carrie is studying to be a teacher in Illinois.

"So, will she be on her way back home?" I ask.

"Oh, heavens no," she replies with a start, "we told her not to come. I do not want her to be here in this dangerous place. I have enough to worry about. I don't need to add her life to the list."

I am so focused on solving this case that I have momentarily forgotten the fear that the family and the people of the town are experiencing. "Mrs. Abbe, that was a smart decision. I would do the same with my children."

She smiles at the compliment, "How are your little ones, Sheriff?"

We talk about my family for a while and both appreciate the all too brief distraction. I catch Alden's impatient eye and remember why we are here.

"Mr. Moorehouse, I would like to introduce you to Major Alden Adams, the Justice of the Peace for Manatee County. Would you please join us to provide your official eyewitness account of the murder?" I saw the familiar look of exhaustion in his eyes.

"Of course," he says as he takes one more drink of water and then properly excuses himself from Mrs. Abbe's breakfast table. We step out on to the Abbe's front porch, and Moorehouse once again recounts Saturday's events to Adams as two of the other men take notes. He shares the same information that he shared with me a couple of days ago, and then we decide to stay here to get Cunliff's testimony as well.

Cunliff begins and shares what he saw that day but pauses, "I have one more thing to add if I may, Sheriff?"

"By all means, we appreciate anything that you would like to add to the record to help solve this case," I reply.

"Well," he hesitates for a moment, "I harbor no ill will towards anyone in Sarasota, but I do think that there was some bad blood between Alfred Bidwell and Charles Abbe. I don't rightly know what it was about, but Bidwell has been vocal about his dislike of Abbe and often tries to persuade others to join him in this point of view. It frustrated him that I would not agree with his harsh statements about Abbe."

"Would you be able to provide an example of the type of things Bidwell has say about Abbe?" I sense a shift in Cunliff; I believe it is the same fear that is creeping through the entire community.

"There are the usual things about Abbe's position as a republican. He also was not fond of the fact that Abbe was appointed postmaster, and he frequently told people that he didn't believe that Abbe received his appointment as Commissioner of the U.S Circuit and District Courts honestly. Now I know that is all rubbish, and I am pretty sure that it came from a place of envy, but there are many men in this area who seem to believe his rants."

Another piece of the puzzle begins to fit in my mind. I knew that the gun was shot from the front of Bidwell's store, that in her panic Charlotte looked there for the body, and that Bidwell had his store closed on a Saturday. But now it seems that, at the very least, Bidwell was the one stirring up the animosity towards Abbe in the town.

With Morehouse's and Cunliff's testimonies complete, I give my official statement to Adams. The group falls silent when I finish, but I don't think it is due to what I had just said. It was because of the task that lay before us.

I take a deep breath and break the silence, "Gentlemen, it is time to head down to the bay and begin our attempt to retrieve the body of Charles Abbe."

~~~~~~~

Major Adams takes one other man and goes to find out if any other members of the town had information about the murder. Cunliff leads Riggin, me, and two other members of our posse to his wharf. He graciously agrees to let us use his skiff and oystering tools to search the bay. He also is the only one who knows which direction Bacon's boat had headed with
~~~~~~~

the body. Cunliff has one oyster rake and managed to borrow two others from people in the town. The long-handled tool was usually used to gather oysters off the bed of the bay, but today we would use it to see if we would be able to find the body of Charles Abbe.

I am walking slightly ahead of the group with Richard when he quietly says, "They are threatening me." He obviously doesn't want to others to hear.

"Who's threatening you?" I ask in a whisper. But by this point, we are at the shoreline and the others have caught up to us. Willard is on the run, so there must be others in town who are trying to protect him. Without the ability to question Richard more, I can only pray that those who are threatening him will be taken away when we make our arrests this evening,

It's early afternoon, almost exactly seventy-two hours since the body had been disrespectfully dragged out to the bay. Based on our clues, we can assume that they dropped the body in the water. I can't imagine that they would have brought it back. The five of us fill the boat, and two of the men begin to row as Cunliff directs.

"I want everyone to be looking carefully at all times," I command. "They likely didn't leave the body in the shallow waters; however, it's been days and the body could have washed back towards shore." They all nod as they hesitantly turn their gazes to the bright water.

The water is clear, the air is pleasant, and the oars make the only sound. Any other time this would be a peaceful day on the bay. I notice that I don't see any birds. The sky is completely clear, not even a cloud in sight. This all adds to the eeriness of our quest.

We had rowed out about 300 feet into the bay when one of the men sees something in the water. We stop the boat and George grabs one of the rakes to drag the bed. The bay is only about five and a half to six feet deep at this spot. We all wait in anticipation as he moves the rake through a large crop of seagrass.

After several minutes, he slowly shakes his head, and I nod at the men to begin rowing again. We stop two more times before we reach the pass that leads to the gulf: once for more seagrass and once for a curious manatee that swam near our boat.

The sun glistens on the horizon as we float through the barrier islands and enter the gulf from the pass. I gaze at the immense body of water and realize the insurmountable task of finding this body. The bay is calm and shallow, seven feet deep at most, but as soon as we emerge on the west side of the keys, the depth sharply increases to twenty then thirty feet. The men who murdered Abbe know this water well; they knew what they were doing when they dropped the body. The men continue to search as I sit and think about how I am going to share this news with Charlotte. Losing Rebecca was terrible, but there is a special closure that comes from being able to say goodbye to her, and I continue to find solace when I visit her grave. How are Charlotte and her children possibly going to be able to move forward without the body?

"Sheriff. Sheriff." I am jolted back to the present moment by Richard's voice. "Yes?" I reply as I shake myself out of my thoughts.

"The sun is starting to set; we should turn around now if we want to make it back to shore before dusk." I nod as the boat turns away from the setting sun. We all continue to investigate the water, but I am sure that everyone has realized that although none of us looked forward to discovering the body, not discovering the body was far worse.

~~~~~~~~

Alden and the rest of the men are waiting near the shore when we return. Some are sitting on the ground, some are meandering and chatting on the street, but none are smiling or laughing.

I shake my head to Alden as I approach to indicate that we did not find the body; he shakes his head in return to let me know that Willard is still on the run.

"We don't have a body, and we do not have our main suspect," Alden states as I walk toward the group from the water, "but at this point I am able to issue warrants for the arrests of Dr. Adam Hunter and Joe Anderson." I turn to watch the remainder of the sun vanish on the horizon and then head to finish today's tasks. I don't mutter a word as I mount my horse. The rest of the group follow on their horses or in their wagons as we first head to the Hunters' home.
~~~~~~~~

It is dark when I knock on the door. Adam Hunter opens the door and drops his head. His wife Virginia calls from inside, "Adam, who's at the door?"

"It's Sheriff Watson, dear. Don't worry, I just need to talk to him." He steps out onto the porch.

"Adam Hunter, you are under arrest for accessory to the murder of Charles Abbe."

"Listen here, Sheriff, there is no way that I would have been able to—" he is cut short by Virginia throwing open the door.

"You do not have enough evidence to take my husband!" she yells. Virginia is a bright woman, but she is not someone I ever want on my bad side.

"Mrs. Hunter, I understand your concerns, but I assure you that we have more than enough evidence to arrest your husband as an accessory. We will treat him with the dignity of the law, and if he had nothing to do with this murder, he will be home soon."

Virginia knows that I am correct, but she continues with her plea. "Sheriff, you don't understand what it's like to live here. You don't understand the pressure . . . the—" This time she is the one who is interrupted by her husband.

He takes her face with his hands, "Ginny, it will be fine." Tears stream from her eyes as she nods in response. He then takes his hands from her face, turns towards me, and lowers them together for his arrest.

The heavy iron handcuffs make a loud click as I clap them around his wrists and turn the key. I had never seen a pair of handcuffs until I was in the war, and now the sound takes me back to a time that I desperately try to forget. I know that there are some who remember the war with fondness—those who felt valiant and righteous—but I was just a young farm boy with no stake in that war, yet I found myself in the trenches.

I was twenty-two years old when I enlisted in the Confederate cavalry. It was a good thing that I had no idea what was in front of me. Honestly, I don't know if I would have gone if I knew the level of death, fear, hunger, and loss that I experienced during my three years of service. And here we are again, people killing over political beliefs. I know that no good can come of this. I wonder if humanity will ever learn to live in harmony despite our differences. Until then, it is my job to maintain as much peace as possible.

Alden and I escort Adam to one of the wagons. He sits quietly as the group heads to the Andersons' home. The easy arrest of Hunter makes me overly confident. Initially, our knocks go unanswered at the Andersons' home.

"Open up, by order of the Manatee County Sheriff!" I yell through the door as we continue to knock.

"Who sent you? Are you listening to that old crow Cunliff?" came the response from within.

"We have multiple testimonies that put you in direct connection with the accused murderer and cite the use of your gun as the murder weapon. You are under arrest as an accessory to murder, Mr. Anderson."

Silence. I look at Alden hoping that he might know how to proceed. The men behind me are getting angry, and I am worried about how they might choose to handle this situation.

"Mr. Anderson, you will be going with us tonight one way or the other. I would prefer a peaceful arrest, but there are twenty-five armed men surrounding your home if you would like to do this the hard way."

The door slowly opens, and Joseph Anderson emerges with his arms held slightly above his head. We load him in the other wagon, and the entire group begin the journey back to the river.

~~~~~~~

The Manatee County jail is way out east in the town of Pine Level. That is a day's trip, at the least, and not something we can embark on at this time. Alden and I decide that the storage room at his commissary will have to serve as the holding cell for now. It is not large, but sufficient for holding the two men. I entrust a couple of men from the posse to stay with them for the night. It is becoming very clear to me that I am going to have to create some more formal positions soon to properly handle this case. The men in the posse mean well, but I think I best get them under oath as soon as possible.

It is well after midnight when I open the door to my house. It is dark and quiet, but I soon hear some rustling upstairs. Clem comes down the stairs and gives me a sympathetic look.
~~~~~~~

"You look like hell," he says with a grin.

"I feel like it too, son," I respond, returning the smile.

"Is there anything I can do for you?" he asks.

"Keeping the family safe is more than enough," I respond. I wash my face and hands, and we both head upstairs to try to get some sleep.

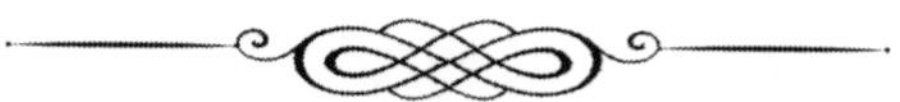

Chapter Six

My body aches as I stir in the morning light. I don't believe I moved at all once my head hit the pillow last night. The house is full of noise and for a moment I am reminded of the sounds on Christmas morning. That was not even a week ago. We aren't used to so much happening in such a short length of time; one of the things I like most about living here is the slow pace of life. I think I will appreciate that pace more than ever when this ordeal is finally over.

As I creep down the stairs, I see that Fannie has breakfast on the table, and everyone is sitting down to eat. She shouldn't be responsible for the family at such a young age, but I don't see myself marrying again anytime soon. I know that most men do in situations like this, since we need help raising the young ones and running the household, but I have not had the desire. Maybe Clem and Fannie make my life too easy; maybe my heart is not willing to risk the pain of possibly losing another wife; maybe I'm too tired to try. Regardless, as I gaze at the children at the table, I think we are doing just fine.

Wade notices me and jumps up from the table so quickly that I think he is going to knock it over. I kneel on the floor as he wraps his arms around my neck. He is closely followed by Will and then the tiny arms of Eva and Alex. I close my eyes and almost fall over in the laughter of the group hug. "Yes," I think to myself, "we are doing just fine."

"How would you all like to take a walk along the river after we clean up our breakfast dishes?" I receive a swell of yeses from the children.

The air is crisp and the is sky bright blue when I load Cliff into his baby carriage. The baby carriage was a gift from Major Adams and his wife after Cliff was born and Rebecca had passed. I sit my hat next to him and lift Eva to her spot, sitting on my shoulders. Fannie pushes the carriage over the sandy roads toward the river. Clem runs ahead with Will and Wade to make sure that they do not get into too much trouble along the way. As we reach the banks of the river, I breathe in the familiar and comforting smell of the water and try to stay present in the moment. It takes a lot of effort to keep the murder case out of my mind, but I need to clear my head if I have any hope of managing this case properly.

We walk west along the river. A new village named Braidentown has recently developed just down the river from Manatee. More and more people have discovered the beauty of this area, and I don't think the growth is going to slow down any time soon. Even more reason why I need to set a high standard of excellence with the quality of this case. There I go, thinking about work again. I turn my attention to the stones and shells that the children have gathered. Before I know it, the sun is almost directly above us, and I realize that we need to head back home.

Clem brings some water in the house, and we all drink heavily. Even though it is December, a person still works up a thirst in the Florida sun.

"I am so happy that you are back," Fannie says as she sets her cup down.

"Well," I reply, "I am only back for the morning, the case is not over." I watch her brown eyes swell with tears, and I realize that she thought this was the end of the ordeal.

I move to her side and place my hands on her shoulders. "I am sorry, dear," I say as the others quiet themselves to listen. "But there is a bad man that is still out there, and we need to find him to keep everyone safe." I don't want to scare them, but I also need them to understand why I must be gone. Little Alex begins to cry, and Fannie hurries to comfort him.

After she has him calm again, she looks up and quietly says, "I understand, Pa."

~~~~~~~~

The guilt I feel leaving the family again is strong, but I know that what I am doing is for the greater good. That's a funny thing, isn't it? The greater good. You can't just pick up a book and look up the answer. It's something that you must feel in your gut. There are these moments in life when you realize that what you are doing affects more than just you. This is one of those moments for me. Life in these parts is tough. I could ignore this murder and let the community work it out on its own, but there is something that I can't explain moving me forward. I feel as if Manatee County is at a crossroads, and I am going to lead them down the path of a greater tomorrow.

It's New Year's Eve. Rebecca loved celebrating the new year. We would sit around the dinner table on December 31,
~~~~~~~~

and she would have everyone reminisce about their favorite things that happened during that year. Then, when we woke up to a new year, we would sit around the breakfast table to talk about what we would be excited about in the upcoming year. I hated to miss this with the children, but I know that Clem and Fannie will keep the tradition alive.

Alden and I agreed to meet this morning at his home. We didn't want to take the chance that we would be overheard in his office. The temperature is lowering a bit, and I have a feeling that a cold front is on its way. The door to the home opens before I knock.

"Major Adams is expecting you. Please follow me." The servant takes my hat and jacket as he leads me through the house back to the room where we had met to first discuss the murder. We both stand facing the river for a few minutes before either of us speaks.

"We have the new warrants," Alden says with his usual composure. We are both still facing the river. There is something universally calming about its steady flow.

"For both Ed Bacon and Alfred Bidwell?" I ask. I realize my voice sounds faint. The gravity of having to arrest two more men is starting to weigh on me.

"Yes, we definitely have enough evidence for both now. It also seems as if we are causing quite a stir throughout the state."

"What do you mean?" It is rare that our small area in the wilderness ever crosses the minds of those in the larger cities.

“Well,” he finally turns to face me as he continues, “a telegram came this morning from a paper up in Ybor City. They asked if they could interview me about, and I quote, our murderous thugs.”

I am stunned that this story has been heard up in that area, but I guess a murder story always sells papers.

“I have been thinking, Alden, we need help. I want to deputize some men to search for Willard. Maybe a dozen or so from the men who joined the posse. Then they can head out to continue looking for Willard, and we can take a couple of others with us back down to Sarasota this afternoon to arrest Bidwell and Bacon.”

“That’s a mighty fine idea, but we need to get a move on. Do you think we can do this all today?”

“Yes. We must.”

~~~~~~~

It didn’t take long to round up ten able-bodied young men that I trust enough to deputize. Once again, young Pliny Reasoner was the first to volunteer. We might have gotten off to a stressful start when he first showed up in Sarasota, but he has proven himself to be smart and dedicated. And, after his anger subsided a bit, a levelheaded thinker as well.

We stand outside of Alden’s store. Alden holds the Bible next to me as we face these ten men. Pliny is standing on the left end of the lineup, next to him is Furman Whitaker, Charles Abbe’s son-in-law, and to his left is Darwin Curry,
~~~~~~~

Arvid's younger brother. All ten of the men are equipped with shotguns, pistols, and rifles—whatever they were able to find.

"Thank you all for your willingness to serve your community. You all understand the risks associated with this hunt. We do not have reason to believe that Charlie Willard is armed, but we do not know how many others have been assisting him in his escape. Every day we are discovering that more people are involved in this sinister plot, so be cautious who you trust. The goal is to bring Willard home alive, so that he can be tried and punished according to the law."

I look up and down the line. All the men are looking right back at me, listening intently. "If any of you would like to change your mind, there is no shame in that. We will all understand and continue to respect you. Would any of you like to back out at this time?" No one even flinches.

Alden moves forward with the Bible and says, "All, please raise your left hand and place your right hand over your heart."

"Repeat after me. I do solemnly swear," I pause, and they state in unison: "I do solemnly swear."

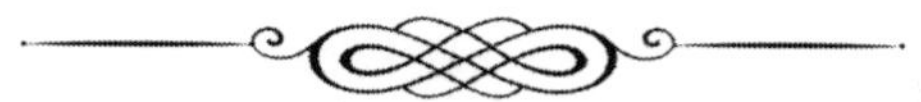

Chapter Seven

After the ten new deputies leave to track down Willard, Alden and I meet up with George and Sam Harris, who had both joined us during the arrest of Anderson and Hunter. I have two more men stationed at our makeshift holding cell to keep watch.

We take two wagons so that we will be able to safely bring back the men. I had made the trip down to Sarasota so many times in the last few days that I am able to avoid some of the low points and brush along the way. It is still a long trip, but at least now we aren't being slowed down as much as we travel. George sits next to me as I drive my wagon, and Sam drives the other with Alden.

"What should we expect when we get down to Sarasota, Sheriff?" When George asks this question, I am reminded of Arvid asking something similar the night of the murder. Although there are still many unanswered questions, I feel much more confident answering now than I did that night.

"Honestly, George," I begin, "my experience with Alfred Bidwell is that he talks big but is really a weak man." George chuckles at this observation. "I think he will come with us easily, that's why we are going to arrest him first. Ed Bacon, on the other hand, I think he's a bit of a hot head."

"I agree with that," George responds. "There are some good people in the Bacon family, but Ed's always been a wild one. Do you think we are going to have to be tough with him?"

"Possibly, but I think we can handle him. We will keep Alden with Bidwell in the wagon and between you and Sam and me, we can take Ed."

"You really have given this a lot of thought, haven't you, Sheriff?"

"It's all I have thought about for days now, George."

It is around 6:00 p.m. that evening when we arrive in Sarasota. It is dark by now and I wish we could have come earlier, but we had to get the others on the road to find Willard. There are so many pieces to this case that nothing is going exactly according to my plan. We start at Bidwell's store first, but it is locked up for the day, so we head out to his house.

Bidwell has a nice two-story home with a large wraparound porch. He's doing all right for himself here in Sarasota, but it is well known that this house is thanks to family money and his wife. We see light inside as we approach, and Alfred is at the door before we even stop.

"Sheriff, I thought I would be seeing you. You can't possibly believe that I had anything to do with this murder, do you?" Alfred starts speaking before I open my mouth. He is waving his arms nervously and stepping off the porch towards our wagons.

The four of us are down on the ground and we met Alfred in his yard. He obviously knows why we are there, so I don't bother with pleasantries.

"Alfred Bidwell, you are under arrest for accessory to the murder of Charles Abbe."

"Now come on, Sheriff, what do you need to make this go away?" I laugh at Bidwell as he changes his tactic from denial to bribery.

"No need for any of that, Bidwell. Please just come with us, and if you are innocent, your name will be cleared in the courts."

"At least allow me to go in and tell my wife and grab my coat." I assume he is up to something, but I don't want to cause this to go badly.

"You are allowed to enter the house, but we will be stationed around the house, and if you are not out in five minutes, we will be coming in." The others look at me like I have lost my mind; maybe I have.

He walks up to the porch. George and Sam go to the back side of the house to keep watch, and Alden and I stay in the front. Surprisingly, Alfred returns quickly with his hands held out. I easily place the cuffs on him. Either he is up to something, or he is actually innocent. My guess is the former.

With Bidwell cuffed and in the wagon, we head to the Bacon home. Once again, our suspect comes out of the house to meet us as we ride up. But unlike Bidwell, Bacon is yelling loudly and flailing his arms as he runs towards us.

I hand the reins to George and quickly jump down off the wagon.

"I know my rights, and you don't have any evidence. And you don't even know the whole story, you Yankee-loving, pathetic excuse for the law."

At this point he is screaming directly at me. I wipe his spit off my face and begin, "Edmund Bacon, you are under arrest for accessory to the murder of Charles Abbe." I roll my eyes as he turns to run and slams right into Sam. In his fit, Ed didn't even see Sam walk up behind him.

Several members of the Bacon family are now out on the lawn with us. I walk up to Ed's father and explain the situation. Alden, who watches wearing a slight grin on his face, is back at the wagon with Bidwell as Sam and George attempt to cuff their squirming suspect. They manage to tie him up, but Ed continues to struggle and yell.

"Mr. Bacon," I address Ed's father, "I regret to inform you that your son is under investigation for the murder of Charles Abbe."

He looks down at his hands and says, "I am mighty sorry, Sheriff."

"Waddy, I place you in high regard and I don't believe that your son's actions are any reflection on you."

He looks up with a tear in his eye and whispers, "Thank you."

I can't imagine how this must feel. I say a silent prayer that I never have to go through anything like this with one of my children.

I walk back to the wagons and am pleased to see that George and Sam have managed to cuff Ed and get him into the back. They decide to keep the extra rope that they had used to restrain him on for good measure.

Alden and Bidwell are both watching from the other wagon. Alden continues to have a smirk on his face, but Bidwell's face is pleading. He shouts over to Ed, "This is not the way. Keep calm." I don't know if Ed didn't hear him or just doesn't care because he continues to yell nonsense into the dark sky.

George and I jump up on the wagon that has Bacon tied in the back while Sam and Alden take Bidwell. I have come to appreciate the quiet time of contemplation as we ride, but there was no peace on this particular part of the journey. Bacon continues to spew ridiculous statements. I should have brought something to stuff in his mouth.

The guards had changed watch at the holding room by the time we arrive to add Bidwell and Bacon to the room with Hunter and Anderson. I thank the guards for their work and make sure that they don't need anything. It's well after midnight when Major Adams and I are finally able to head to our homes.

"Happy New Year, Sandy."

"Happy New Year to you, Alden."

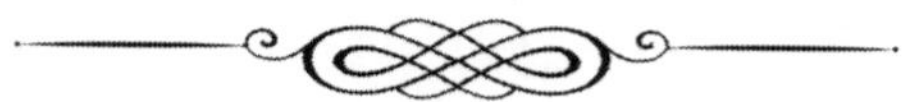

Chapter Eight

Once again, the children are all in bed by the time I enter the house that night, but I am still the first one awake. The overwhelming fatigue that had allowed me to sleep at the beginning of this case is no longer helping, and I just can't manage to rest. This is not the way I had planned to start 1885.

I boil some water for coffee and sit down at the table when I hear some quiet footsteps. "Good morning, Fannie," I say before turning around. None of the others are capable of being that quiet.

"I am so happy to see you, Pa." Her smile stretches all the way across her small face. She crawls into my lap and rests her head on my shoulder. "Are we going to go see Ma today?" she asks.

New Year's Day 1884 had been our first without Rebecca, so we went as a family to her gravesite. I guess Fannie wants to make it a tradition. "I think that is an excellent idea, sweetheart. We will go after breakfast."

"Thank you." She kisses my cheek, jumps off my lap, and begins breakfast. I take a sip of my coffee and join her.

"Pa, did you catch all the murderers? Are we all safe now?" I hate to see her frightened, but I also believe it is important to be honest with my children. They aren't going to survive long in this world if I shelter them from reality.

"Almost. We still have one more. He took off running like a coward and now my new deputies are searching for him."

"You have new deputies?" She is much more excited about this than the fugitive on the run. "Who are they?" she asks excitedly. I name all ten for her.

"Darwin!" She giggles and I see her blush a bit. Is it possible that my daughter has a bit of a crush on one of the Curry boys?

"Yes, Darwin is one of the new deputies. Do you like him?"

"Oh, Pa!" she exclaims and turns to set the table, so that I can't see her smile. Clem finally comes down to join us.

"Sorry, Pa. I don't know why I slept in so late."

"Because you now know how tiring it is to run a household." He gives an exaggerated nod. And then the chaos begins. Fannie leaves the room to get Clifford and Eva while the twins and little Alex tell me all their stories from during my absence.

It is around nine o'clock when the eight of us enter the burying grounds. We took the carriage for both Eva and Cliff to sit in and a blanket for the rest of us. Clem spreads the blanket out in front of his mother's stone while Fannie positions the pram next to it.

"Will! Wade!" I try to make my voice as stern as possible while still being respectably quiet. "Do not forget your manners. This is a place of contemplation."

"Pa," Will looks up at me very seriously, "we don't know what that means." I smile down at him and put my hand on his shoulder. We sit on the blanket, and I explain the word *contemplation* to the boys the best I am able.

We sit for a while in silence and then Clem begins telling fun stories about his mother. I know some families don't talk much about those who have passed, but I want my children to remember her. Soon the youngest children get restless, and Clem offers to walk them around the cemetery. Will and Wade decide to join him.

"Don't worry," says Wade, "we promise to be contemplately."

"No, Wade," Will interrupts, "it's contemplotive." I smile as they walk away deep in conversation.

Fannie is still sitting on the blanket with me. "Do you want to walk around?" I ask her.

"No, thank you." Her brow is deeply furrowed as she gazes at her mother's stone. She has too much on the mind for a ten-year-old.

"Is there anything you would like to talk about?" I ask.

"Why do people do bad things?" She continues to stare at the grave. I know that she is truly asking this question of her mother. I say a quick prayer for guidance in my answer.

"I don't know why; I just know that they do. There are mysteries about this world that we simply are not able to understand."

"Then what can we do about it? How can we stop it?"

"All we can do is be good and provide an example to others. You provide one of the best examples for your little brothers and sister because you are so good. And that is a lot, Fannie." She looks up at me and smiles. Clem returns with the others, and we pack up to head back home.

~~~~~~~

As soon as we unpack at the house, it is time for me to check on the guards and the prisoners. I ride up to town and see that a large crowd has now gathered outside of the building where the suspects are being held. They fill the sidewalk and spill onto the street, talking loudly and threatening to take matters into their own hands. I try to calm them down, talk some sense into the group, but they have become a mob and I can no longer be heard over their shouting.

I walk to the center of the road, draw my pistol from the holster, aim it straight into the sky, and pull the trigger.

"Enough!" I shout as the crowd hushes to the sound of the shot. "We will trust in the law, and we will conduct a proper trial. If we do not, then we are no better than the scoundrels that are being held."
~~~~~~~

"Sheriff!" I turn slightly to glimpse Major Adams standing behind me. "We need to talk."

The crowd begins to murmur among themselves again, but the threat level had been subdued for the moment. I nod to my terrified deputies as I enter the building behind Alden.

We walk to his office and close the door. "What came over you, Sandy? That was a dangerous move."

"They don't understand, and they won't listen!" I was still agitated by the crowd but was beginning to see the gravity of my action.

"Of course, they won't listen. They are a mob, they are angry, and although none of them will admit this, they are frightened. But it is not your job to lose your temper, it is your job to lead them. So, what are you going to do now?"

I sit on the wooden chair in front of Alden's desk. It seems to creak under the weight of my thoughts. The clock ticks on the wall, and the murmurs begin to grow louder outside again.

I take a few deep breaths to calm myself and then say with as much confidence as I can muster, "Major Adams, I am moving the prisoners."

He gazes at me and for a moment I wish I could retract my statement. But slowly a grin forms under his thick mustache. "Well, Sheriff, I think that is a solid plan."

I finally exhale the deep breath that I didn't realize I was holding. "Alden, how do you do it? How do you keep your composure during these times?"

He sits on the corner of his desk nearest me, and his eyes grow thoughtful. This is a side of him I had not seen before. "Sandy," he begins, "why are you here?"

"What do you mean? I am here because I am the sheriff, and it is my job."

"I mean, *here*, in the wilderness of Florida."

"Because, I had nothing left back home. Because I wanted a new start, a better life for my family. And somewhere during my quest for a new start, I fell in love with this place. And now it is my home. My children were born here, my Rebecca is buried here, and I am going to do everything within my power to ensure that this is a home that they all deserve."

"And there is your answer. I am able to compose myself during these trying times because the people and the place that I call home deserve the best future possible."

"But they aren't always the most . . ." I glance out the window at the angry people still pacing in front of the office, "the most . . . friendly, are they?"

"You are talking to a Union major living in the south who speaks several foreign languages and keeps exotic animals in his yard." His usual mischievous smile returns to his face. "I am aware that they are not always friendly. Humans have flaws, but in the end, I do think that it is worth it, don't you?" I nod in agreement.

"Now!" he exclaims as he stands up from his desk and stomps one foot on the hard floor. "What shall we do with our friendly mob?" I couldn't help but chuckle. It was the first time I had laughed in days.

~~~~~~~

I walk over to the guards that stand in front of the room holding the suspects and inform them that we are moving the prisoners.

"But where will you take them?" One of them asks with concern.

"To the old warehouse on the wharf. I will post guards at the shore and at the warehouse and the water will provide a barrier between them and the mob."

I open the door to our makeshift holding cell. Bidwell is sitting on one of the wooden chairs we have provided. Hunter is pacing back and forth. Anderson and Bacon are having a quiet conversation.

"Men," I begin.

"Did you finally come to your senses? Are you letting us out?" Ed, of course, had a few things to say.

"No, you are not being released. But a group of upset citizens has gathered, and I am moving you to a safer location.
~~~~~~~

We need to gather more men to help keep the crowd at bay to move you. So, it will take place in an hour or so."

"Thank you," Adam Hunter says softly. Ed gives him a dirty look.

Alden and I gather four more local men to help keep the mob back during the move. The two guards help Alden and me restrain the prisoners. We only have three sets of working handcuffs, so we decide that Bidwell would be the one who we tie with rope. He hasn't been too much trouble and he's a portly man; I am confident that we would be able to capture him quickly if he attempts to run.

We bring two wagons to the back door of the Alden's shop. One guard escorts Bacon and one escorts Anderson to the wagons. I had instructed that they are placed in separate wagons. Those men are the two that I trust the least, and I don't want to give them an opportunity to do something stupid.

Alden and I wait until they are secure in the wagons, and then we bring Bidwell and Hunter out. The mob is staying back, but they are still angry and yelling. For the first time since we have arrested him, Bacon is keeping his mouth shut.

We drive the wagons out along the wharf to the old warehouse building. The mob has followed, but they have remained a respectable distance behind us and listen to the men who instruct them to stay on the mainland. Alden, the guards, and I each help one prisoner off the wagons at a time and walk them into the dim warehouse. Slivers of light come in through the windows at the top of the building. The sound of the water hitting the dock can be heard faintly beneath the floorboards.

A few chairs, a table, and some old orange crates are scattered around the large room. One of the guards heads back out of the building to get the bedticks that we brought along from the last holding cell.

"I think this will do nicely," I say to Alden. I then turn to our prisoners, "We hope that you will not have to be here for long. Major Adams will be subpoenaing witnesses today, and we will find Willard soon. Then we will move you out to Pine Level to await your trial." They all nod. It's interesting how an angry mob can knock the confidence out of scoundrels.

Chapter Nine

It's Sunday morning and four days since the search party left to track down Willard. I know they have a lot of ground to cover, but as I sit in church with my family, his capture is my only prayer.

All things considered, the investigation is moving along at a relatively quick pace. I continue to coordinate the guards at the wharf. The prisoners and the townsfolk have been relatively quiet since I moved the holding cell out there. Major Adams has issued witness subpoenas throughout the county and preliminary judicial examinations are to begin on Tuesday, only ten days after the murder.

I would say that there is one person who is quite pleased with all the commotion. Josiah Gates's hotel is full of witnesses coming to the area on Monday to be ready for their judicial examination on Tuesday.

I awake Tuesday morning knowing that we have a dozen or so testimonies to record from people who know the accused. Alden and a scribe begin taking testimony in his office as soon as the sun rises. I am scheduled to be the final testimony of the day. It is already dark by the time I walk in. George Riggin had testified before me, and I meet him in passing.

"How's it going?" I ask him.

He chuckles, “I think we are going to have to replace the scribe’s hand. He has been writing nonstop all day long.”

Alden looks up when I enter the room, I see relief flash across his face. The scribe is rotating his wrist while massaging it with his other hand.

“Ah, Sandy, that means we have made it to the final testimony of the day.” Alden stands up to stretch his back.

“How’s the day gone? Did you learn anything new?”

“Same stories that we’ve heard before, but now they have been perfectly recorded for all of history.” Alden smiles slyly at the clerk who is too tired to respond to the jest. “Shall we get started, Sheriff?”

I sit down and begin to slowly tell my account again. As I recall the events, the same questions keep running through my mind. How could this have simply been a political rivalry? Why was Willard using Anderson’s gun? Why did Bidwell close his store early that day? Why did Bacon have the boat ready? But if this was orchestrated, then why in the middle of the afternoon in front of witnesses? My gut tells me that there is something else that we need to uncover. Something sinister is still being hidden in Sarasota.

~~~~~~~

Wednesday morning the children and I are sitting down for breakfast when I hear a knock on the door. One of the guards from down at the wharf has come to alert me that Dr. Adam Hunter would like to speak to me in private. I tell the
~~~~~~~

guard to move Hunter to Major Adam's office and I will be there momentarily. I kiss all the little heads on my way out the door. Will and Wade make faces when I do this, but they are still young enough that they put up with it.

"I was told you wanted to talk to me alone," I say gruffly. My patience has worn quite thin throughout this ordeal, and I am not pleased that I had to cut my time with the children short.

"Yes, I . . . uh . . . I. Yes," Dr. Adam Hunter stammered. He is standing partially facing me but looking at the wall. It is not like him to be so flustered. He is usually quite articulate. I notice his chin quiver under his beard. I did not know what he wanted to tell me, but I was growing more curious by the moment.

I soften my tone a bit in hopes that it would help ease his fears. "You can trust me, Adam. I want to help." He begins to pace, wringing his hands. He opens his mouth to speak and then tightly closes his lips again and again. He has not made eye contact with me since I entered the room.

Finally, he stops, looks me in directly in the eyes, and says, "Promise me, Sheriff. Promise me that you will keep Virginia and the children safe." The intensity in his voice takes me aback.

"Of course, Adam. No matter what you have to tell me, I promise that I will do everything within my power to keep your family safe."

His eyes drop down to the floor, and he begins to speak slowly. "A man's word means a whole lot, you see. And it means even more when you are settling a new area like we are in Sarasota. You must be able to depend on your neighbors. Do you understand, Sheriff?"

"Yes," I reply, "I definitely understand the honor of one's word." I don't ask any questions. Whatever this is, he needs to share it in his own words and in his own time.

Adam swallows hard, looks out of one of the windows, and continues. "You see, we took an oath. So that's why this is so hard to tell you. And breaking that oath might cost me my life." His entire body trembles. So did mine. "We have a group; we call ourselves the Sarasota Vigilance Committee. The purpose of this group is to maintain our political control. Lots of new folks are coming to the area and many are not of the same mind as us."

I nod and move slightly closer to hear him better. He is still speaking in hushed tones and the poor lighting made it difficult to read his expression. "So, the group started with good intentions. We wanted to ensure that we continue to create the community that we loved. But then things took a turn. That's when I told them I could no longer be part of it." He sits down on one of the wooden chairs in the room. He is quiet for so long that I don't know if he will continue.

"What kind of turn?" I ask after what felt like an eternity of silence.

His voice cracks, and I realize he is in tears. "No one deserved to die."

"Did this group kill Charles Abbe?" I feel a chill run down my spine as he slowly nods his head.

"How many of you are in this group?" I ask.

"Well," he responds, "I'd say about twenty to twenty-five people at this point." I was not anticipating that many. "But like I said, Sheriff, I am not part of the group anymore."

"Do they all support murder?"

"I wouldn't say support, but I don't know of anyone who tried to stop it." His voice raises, "Our lives are threatened. Our families are threatened. It didn't start out this way." He is almost yelling at this point, "It just got out of control."

"But why are people still supporting this organization after realizing what they are truly doing?" I ask completely baffled.

"Like I say, Sheriff, we made an oath. For many of us, our word is all that we've got." He replies with complete sincerity. "And also, we didn't want to be next on the judges' list."

"Who are these judges that you refer to?"

"At the risk of my life, Sheriff, I will share the structure of the organization." After another deep breath, he begins. "The duty of the judges is to consult and determine what parties are to perish. Then there is the captain, he is the enforcer, he executes the judges' orders and punishes the members of the group that don't comply. Beneath him are two lieutenants."

I wait for him to provide those names, but it became clear that he thinks he is finished. "Adam," I move right in front of him and look him directly in the eyes, "you need to tell me who they are."

"I know, Sheriff. I know." He again falls silent.

"Adam," I raise my voice and stand tall, "you say that you joined this group to create the Sarasota that you envisioned. Is that vision of a town full of fear where murderers run free, or is that a future where everyone is safe and prosperous?"

He looks up to me with tears in his eyes, "Alfred Bidwell and Dr. Leonard Andrews are the judges, Jason Alford is the captain, and the lieutenants are Louis Cato and Charlie Willard."

"Thank you, Adam. I know how hard that was for you, but you have saved lives and quite possibly the future of your community."

"My family?" he asks.

"I will have a deputy assigned to ensure they're safe," I reply.

I walk out into the sunshine. It is blinding after being in that dark room, or maybe it was just the blinding light of reality. How is this possible? These are well-respected men. But I guess that's why it was possible. They have a strong influence over people. I just didn't know how strong that influence was. I had so many questions that I wanted to ask him, but I also had work that needed to be done immediately. I am sure that more is going to be revealed during the trial.

The guard who accompanied Hunter looks at me curiously, I know that he is anxious to hear what I had been told, but the look on my face must have stopped him from asking.

"Keep Dr. Hunter locked up in this space. Stand on guard until you hear word from me." He nods and stays silent.

I mount my horse and start towards Alden's home.

~~~~~~~

I once again join Alden in the back room of his home. The calm, flowing river before us is not able to stop my hands from trembling.

"Sandy," Alden says with concern, "what has happened to put you in this state?" After all we have been through the past couple of weeks, he knows that it would take a lot to make me this upset.

"Dr. Hunter asked to see me in private this morning." Alden is listening intently. "He informed me of an organized group in Sarasota that murders." Alden stands looking out to the river in silence.

"Did you learn anything else?" I tell him the names of the leaders. His eyes grow wide, and he does not move. He is clearly in shock.
~~~~~~~

He finally speaks, “Well, we need a plan.” I am surprised that he doesn’t ask any more questions or have anything else to say about this revelation. But I realize that creating a plan is what he does best and right now he is sticking with that.

Alden is going to get Dr. Hunter’s official confession and then we plan to leave him in the storage room at Alden’s office. Who knows what those rats would do to him if they had any inkling that he confessed? We are planning to take the prisoners to the jail out in Pine Level tomorrow anyway. I step out of the front door of Alden’s home to get to work.

The weather has begun to turn. You can always feel the shift, the sun is hidden behind some clouds, the humidity has lifted, and the breeze is now strong enough to rustle the leaves in the trees. As I listen to the leaves in the wind, I hear another sound. The sound of hooves. I see a horse rapidly approaching. It’s Pliny Reasoner. I hold my breath and hope for good news. I can hear him yelling before he reaches the house.

“We got him! We got him!” he yells joyously.

I turn to Alden’s servant who is still in the doorway behind me, “Fetch the Major! We finally have some good news!”

Pliny dismounts from his horse and the door crashes behind me as Alden barrels through it. He runs past me and rushes to Pliny in the yard.

Pliny’s clothing is torn, his boots are so caked with mud that you can’t even see the color, his hands are cut and bloody, his face is covered in dirt, his eyes are bloodshot, but his grin still covers his entire face.

"Willard's being taken to Pine Level. He's half dead, but at least he will have to stand trial. Along the way, we heard that this wasn't the first white man he's killed. It's about time he faces the consequences for all of his evil deeds."

"Well done, Pliny." Alden and I both take our turn shaking his hand and patting his back.

Pliny continues to share the story, "We headed south first to search around Yonge's again. Then we forded the creek to get to Robinson's homestead. We weren't having any luck, so we decided to head out to Sheppard's camp on Myakka River since he is known to be a friend of Willard."

Pliny takes a seat on the steps of the porch and one of Alden's servants steps out of the house, holding a tray with three glasses of lemonade. Pliny drinks his down quickly and politely requests another. I give him the glass that had been intended for me.

"We stopped at every house along the way. Most people didn't know the whole story and were afraid we were just out to lynch Willard, but once we showed them our deputy orders, they paid attention." Pliny stops for another drink.

"Gus Wilson told us that Willard had stopped by begging him for a horse. Gus didn't know what Willard had done or he would have apprehended him right then and there. Good thing he knew better than to give him a horse, or this story would have had a very different ending."

He continues, "Anyway, we headed up to Smallwood's place and continued to search high and low. We knew we were on the right track; we just couldn't catch up to him. In the end, it was Sheppard who found him and convinced him to surrender."

"I just don't have words enough to thank you all for what you did, Pliny," I say with pure respect and admiration. "That was a harrowing journey, and you brought a potential murderer to justice."

I couldn't share with Pliny all the other information that I had learned that morning, but I am sure he will recognize the significance soon enough. The sun had set at this point, and we are basking in the glow of twilight. The cool air is blowing in hard now and tomorrow is going to be a cold one, well, cold by our standards.

After Pliny leaves, I say goodbye to Alden. "Well, that was another unexpected day. Hopefully, tomorrow will be less eventful."

"This is no time to be jinxing us, Sandy." He waves as he goes back into his home.

~~~~~~~

It continues to grow colder, so Clem and I start a fire in the hearth and pull out the extra blankets from the chest. Fannie takes the littlest ones into bed with her, and Clem even jumps into bed with Will and Wade. It is definitely a cold night when that happens!
~~~~~~~

I tell them all about the heroic work of our deputies and ease their minds with the fact that Willard is now in jail. But, of course, I must keep quiet about Dr. Hunter's confession.

I sit at the table and stare at the fire. It crackles occasionally and the wind is echoing through the house, but my thoughts are drowning out all the noises. One moment I feel grateful and proud of the deputies who tracked down Willard. And, if I am being honest with myself, I am slightly proud of myself for the way that I have handled this case thus far. I have trusted my gut, and it has not led me astray.

But then I think about this committee and the havoc they have wreaked upon innocent civilians. I think about Charlotte standing tall in her mourning attire behind the post office counter. I think about the fact that she will never have the closure of holding a wake for her husband.

How did a difference in political views turn to cold-blooded murder? I have seen war, but it's different somehow, right? Major Adams and I fought for opposing sides and here we are now working together for the common good.

But what if we had met on the battlefield? I shudder at the thought.

Chapter Ten

The temperature continues to drop throughout the night. We must leave before sunrise to get the prisoners to the jail in Pine Level by dark.

I decide to take four guards and a driver with me on the trip. One guard for each prisoner and an extra if needed. The six of us meet at the end of the pier and walk through the chilly, damp air toward warehouse together. As soon as we open the door, Ed Bacon begins to rant.

"Where is that old Hunter? He squealed, didn't he? I knew he couldn't be trusted! I told you all that he was not one of us! He's going to pay for this!"

I ignore him and the others follow my example. I know there is nothing that will calm him down at the moment. Alden and I had decided that it would not be safe to have Dr. Hunter in the wagon or in the prison with the others anymore, so he will continue to be guarded here.

We handcuff the prisoners' hands behind their backs, walk them along the pier to the shore, and load them into the wagon. We don't have extra coats for them, but we do have a few horse blankets to keep them warm. Will is going to drive the wagon. He had only moved here a couple of years ago from Indiana, and he still likes to jest with us about our intolerance to cold. I am sure his pride won't let him complain about the weather on this journey. I sit up front with Will, and the four guards mount their horses to ride on both sides of the wagon.

We head east to begin the long day's journey. The cold mist has made the road damp and muffles the sound of the horses' hooves. The Village of Manatee is small, and we are soon riding in the open marsh area. This will be our view until we get out to Pine Level. Bacon continues his obnoxious rant, but even he gets tired of talking a few hours into the ride.

We are all silent by the time sun rises over the foggy horizon.

"If it's all right with all of you, I would like to make myself comfortable and rest for a while." Alfred Bidwell breaks the eerie silence.

"That would be fine," I respond and nod to George, his designated guard.

"Would you be ever so kind as to place my handcuffs in the front so I can relax," he asks.

If Anderson or Bacon had asked this question, it would have been a definite no; but Bidwell is too unfit to be a physical threat, so I nod to George again. Will stops the wagon and George dismounts from his horse to unlock Bidwell's cuffs. Bidwell cooperates by placing his hands in front of his body and George easily locks them back into place. Bidwell pulls the blanket up over his head and leans against the sideboard to rest. We continue in silence for a time until Bidwell become restless.

"What's happening back there?" I ask.

"Just getting comfortable," Bidwell responds from under the blanket.

"Stop the wagon!" George yells.

Will pulls the reins to stop the horses, and I quickly jump into the back of the wagon.

"He's swallowed morphine!" George holds up the small, empty, brown bottle.

"You coward!" I scream with anger as I pull Bidwell up by his collar and prop him into a sitting position.

Bacon begins to laugh hysterically. Will is calming the horses, who are startled by the commotion and the bouncing of the wagon. I pull my pistol and point it at Bacon. "Shut up," I say calmly as I stare straight into his eyes. He spits but doesn't speak. He knows I have a bigger problem than him now.

Bidwell is still conscious but not able to speak. His head bobs back and forth as George and I pull him of off the wagon. If he truly consumed that entire bottle, then this is a deadly dose. Without any ipecac to cause him to regurgitate the morphine, there is only one way to prevent this suicide. We lower Bidwell to his knees. George holds him by the shoulders and leans him forward. I put my fingers down his throat and gag him until he empties his stomach.

Will brings us some water and, in his still groggy state, Bidwell drinks heavily. I have so much to say, but we are all under the watchful eyes of the other two prisoners, so I simply load Bidwell back on the wagon. And we continue toward the jail.

I look around at the vast emptiness that surrounds us and think about all the hours left until we reach our destination. There is not another living creature in sight; although, I am sure that there are alligators in the small body of water up ahead. If I weren't a noble man, I would consider dumping all three of them in there to check on the gators.

~~~~~~~

It is dusk when we finally arrive at the jail in Pine Level. The sun gave us a little respite during the day, but as it drops back down below the horizon behind us, I button up my coat to block out the chill. I am physically and mentally exhausted-- and although I try to keep my emotions separate from my work, I am emotionally exhausted from today's journey. I look around at our group and note that everyone looks like I feel.

The town of Pine Level is growing a bit thanks to the railroad announcing that they would be laying track out here within the next year, but the landscape is still quite sparse. It baffles me as to why they decided to move the Manatee County seat way out here. That decision was made shortly before Rebecca and I moved to the area. The official story is that it was because of its central location, but talk in town is that it was a political move. That wouldn't surprise me.
~~~~~~~

The jail is out in the open surrounded by some low brush and one straggly tree. They didn't even bother to use iron in the jail; instead, they built a small two-story building that is entered by a ladder to the second floor. Then the prisoners have to go through a door in the floor and use a ladder to climb down into their cells. They claim that the floors in the cells are a strong double layer of wooden planks to prevent prisoners from digging out, but anyone with half a mind could look at that building and know that a determined prisoner could easily find a way. Even though the prisoners are now under the watch of the warden and his team, I am still the sheriff, and I do not want these bastards escaping.

The Pine Level warden is there to meet us. I shake his hand and thank him for taking it from here. He and two of his guards help the prisoners from the wagon and walk them up the ladder and into the jail. George takes the horses around to the small stable in the back.

I walk over to the jail after the prisoners have been escorted to their cells. I climb up the ladder and enter the door on the second level.

"Excuse me," I ask of one of the guards, "which cell is Charlie Willard in?" The guard knocks on the door in the floor on my left with the end of his shotgun.

"Would you like to see him?" he asks.

"Yes." He pulls a key ring from his pocket and bends down to unlock the cell. He lifts the door on the floor, and I get down on my knees to peer inside.

"Willard?" I yell into the small dark hole.

"Yeah," a faint voice responds. I look closely to see his body slumped in the corner. I can make out a water pitcher and latrine pot, but nothing else.

"Lock it back up," I instruct the guard. "I just needed to see him in there."

With the prisoners secure—well, as secure as a wooden jail could be—in their cells, I descend the ladder and walk away from the building to stare up at the stars. It is downright cold and dark at this point, and the only sound I hear is an owl in the oak tree behind me. I smile in his direction and hope that the common belief that owls symbolize wisdom is true. We are going to need all the wisdom we can get for this trial.

There are only two buildings near the jail, the courthouse and the Methodist Church. I assume we will be able to stay in one of those for the night. Normally we would have been able to sleep in the wagon, but it is just too cold tonight. The warden approaches from the direction of the jail.

"You weren't kidding when you told me that you had a couple of lively ones," he chuckles. "That Bacon kid doesn't know when to shut his mouth!" I laugh, grateful that I will get some relief from his constant nonsense. "The cells are mighty small, so we gave them each their own. But they are still able to talk through the walls."

"You are going to have to keep an eye on Bidwell; he tried to kill himself with morphine during the trip."

“What the hell! Where did he even get that stuff?”

“I guess he had it on him this entire time just waiting for a moment when he thought he could get away with it. But I wasn’t about to let him take the coward’s way out. He is going to be held responsible for his part in this.”

“We’ve been hearing a lot of stories out in these parts about what’s happening down in Sarasota. People are scared, Sheriff. Is it really as bad as the gossip sounds?”

I look back up at the stars, and the owl hoots in the tree. “Yes,” I say, “I think it is actually worse than we know.”

As my gaze comes down, I spy another figure approaching. “Good evening, Pastor,” the warden says.

“Good evening.” The pastor greets us both and waves kindly at the rest of the men who are relaxing near the wagon.

“Sheriff Watson, I presume.”

“Yes, Pastor. It is a pleasure to meet you.” I shake his hand.

“I wanted to thank you for your work in apprehending these godless men and offer you and your team a place to sleep in the church. We have a warm fire already burning.”

“Thank you, Pastor, we would truly appreciate that.”

“Please make yourself at home. I am going over to the jail to pray with the prisoners.”

I watch in admiration as he walks through the dark to try to bring a little light to the prisoners. God knows I don't have the compassion to do that at this moment.

"Well," I turn back to the warden, "I thank you for all of your work, but this has been quite a long day and I think my men and I are going to truly enjoy the fire in the church."

We shake hands once more, and I walk to the wagon to gather the others and head to the warmth of the building. I hear the owl once more as I close the heavy church door.

Chapter Eleven

It has been nearly a week since we left the four prisoners in the jail out at Pine Level. So far, I have not received any notices from the warden, and I take that as a sign that everything is going well. They appointed a new postmaster down in Sarasota, a man by the name of Sam Corwin. I am relieved to hear that. I hope that Charles's family can finally take some time to grieve.

It had been an uneventful morning and the three youngest are upstairs napping. Fannie and the twins burst into the house after a day at school.

"Excuse me, Will and Wade, is that where your books belong?"

"Sorry, Pa!" they yell in unison as they grab the books that they had dropped on the floor.

"And not so loud, the little ones are sleeping."

"Pa," Fannie begins excitedly, "I can't wait to tell you what we learned about in school today!"

"What?" I love her enthusiasm for learning.

"France! Have you ever heard of it? It sounds lovely! I want to go there someday!"

"Did you know that Major Adams once lived there?"

"Really?" Her eyes widen. "Do you think he has pictures? Would he tell me more about it?"

"I am sure that he would love to talk to you about France. He even speaks French!"

"Maybe after I talk to him, I can give a report about it at school."

"Wait," Wade chimes in, "are you making homework for yourself?"

"Lock her up, Pa; she's crazy," adds Will. The twins giggle as Fannie chases them around the kitchen.

I miss the knock on the door over the ruckus, but then I see a shadow on the porch.

I open the door to see one of Major Adam's servants.

"Sheriff Watson," he states formally, "the Major requests your immediate presence for an urgent matter."

"I know," Fannie says behind me, "watch the kids." I kiss the top of her head, grab my hat and coat from the hook by the door, and leave the family once more.

~~~~~~~

The walk, through Alden's home to the back porch, is familiar to me now. He prefers to take all guests into that
~~~~~~~

space; I think it's because the river provides him with the peace he needs for these difficult conversations.

When I enter the porch, Alden and another man are standing facing the river with their backs towards me. I don't recognize the second man at first, but then he turns around.

"Henry Hawkins?" I know it's him, but I am so confused as to why he is here.

"Sandy, Henry is here on behalf of his father-in-law. He has more information."

"About the Abbe murder?"

"No," Henry says softly, "about the Tip Riley murder."

I remember that murder well, it had happened last summer. It seemed like a cut and dried case. I didn't investigate.

"What?" I silently pray that I had misheard him. "Was that murder part of the Vigilance Committee?"

Henry nods slowly. "Sheriff, I am risking the life of myself and my family coming here today."

"I appreciate your honor, Henry, and I will do everything within my power to keep you and your family safe." I have been making that promise a lot lately.

He continues, "The group's first murder was Harrison Tip Riley." At this point my mind feels like when the twins set up a line of dominos just to watch them topple over in a chain reaction. The pieces are now fitting together. I try to remain as calm as possible so that Henry will continue speaking.

Henry goes on to corroborate everything that Adam Hunter had told us.

I decide it is time to ask the big question. “Did they kill anyone other than Riley and Abbe?”

“Not that I know of, but there is a list. After Riley’s murder went off without any consequences, the judges decided to take the number one person off the list.” My heart sinks into my feet as the reality of the situation clarifies. This murder happened because I did not investigate Riley’s death. My confidence begins to crumble, but then I remember that there are more people on this list—people who I must protect. My sense of duty returns like a lion.

After Henry has completed his statement, Alden fetches someone to bring pen and paper and they write the affidavit for Henry to sign.

We thank Henry again for his bravery as we walk him to the front door.

“Well, now I think that we need to—” as usual Alden moves right into planning.

I cut him off, “I’m sorry, Alden. I have a couple of things I need to do right now.”

“Now?” I hear him ask from the doorway, but I am already on my way to my horse.

~~~~~~~

I enter the burying ground and walk the familiar path to Rebecca's final resting spot. With my hat in my hands, I bow my head and gaze at the headstone.

"Rebecca," I begin, "I failed. You remember Tip Riley, don't you? Well, he was murdered last summer. He was murdered and I, the sheriff of Manatee County, did not investigate." I take a deep breath and turn my head upward towards the Spanish moss swaying overhead in the oak tree. "I just thought, he had it coming. He was living in sin with a widow. He had made a lot of enemies, but it was my job, Becky. I took an oath to uphold the law of this county, and I didn't do it. And now, because of my failure, another innocent man is dead. If only you were here. You would have never allowed me to ignore a murder." I then fall to my knees and drop my hat on the ground. "I am so sorry," I sob.

I notice the dried sprig of beautyberry at the base of the stone as I pick up my hat and dust it off. I take a deep breath. Failure or not, I know what Rebecca would have said to me. She would have told me to get up off the ground and get to work.

~~~~~~~

My next stop is the wharf where we are now holding Dr. Hunter. Although the rumblings in the community about lynching have subsided a bit, that is still a threat to Hunter. And, if word gets out about his confession, that will make him the target of the Vigilance Committee as well. I don't know what he plans to do when all of this is over, but if I were him, I would quickly get out of town.

I nod at the guard stationed at the end of the pier. Adam isn't a flight risk, and even if he did try, I think one guard could handle him. The sound of my boots on the wooden planks echoes slightly under the pier.

I unlock the door and walk in. The room is dark, but the setting sun is creating a bright streak across the room through a space between boards on the west wall.

Hunter is sitting on a wooden chair. I pick up another chair and move it to sit across from him.

"To what do I owe this visit, Sheriff," Adam says calmly. His demeanor has changed dramatically since his confession. I am not sure if it is due to relief or acceptance of his fate.

"We received another statement naming the Vigilance Committee behind the murder of Tip Riley. Do you know anything about that?"

"I had heard something about it, but—like I said—I was no longer part of the group, so I didn't have any firsthand information to report. Also," he pauses, "I didn't think you were concerned with that case." He looks me directly in the eyes when he says this.

"The motive seemed clear; I had no idea that there was a group of murderers behind it."

"Would that have made a difference in your response?" Adam uses my silence as an opportunity to continue. "Sheriff, are you concerned that you are not very different from the leaders of this group?"

I take the bait. "How so?"

"You also feel that you have the authority to judge the value of a human life."

I stand up and walk out of the warehouse.

~~~~~~~

Over the next few days Alden and I are very busy taking statements. I was nervous when news got around about Henry coming to us with information, but the best possible scenario occurred—others mustered up the nerve to do the same. The multiple accounts provided us with enough information to issue warrants for Louis Cato, Coop Brown, and Tom Dryman. I sent others to arrest Cato and Brown, but I decided to go to the Drymans' home myself.

Tom Dryman answers the door slowly. At the sight of me, he drops his eyes to the ground and murmurs what I think is hello, but it is hard to understand. His brother Frank walks up behind him. Tom has been living at Frank's home since the farm accident many years ago.

"How can we help you, Sheriff?" Frank asks.

"Tom," I say, "I am here to arrest you for the murder of Harrison Tip Riley. Do you understand?" He nods his head
~~~~~~~

slowly but never makes eye contact. Since the accident, Tom has not been the same. He is slow to comprehend, slow to speak, and unable to hold a job.

"Surely, there must be some mistake," his brother Frank cries, "Tom wouldn't hurt a fly! May I please talk to him for a moment?"

I nod and watch as Frank takes Tom to the corner of the room and looks him in the eye. I could not hear their conversation, but in this situation, I feel they deserve their privacy.

Frank slowly walks back to me with Tom close behind. Frank simply nods sorrowfully, and I put my hand on Tom's shoulder to lead him out to the wagon. He comes willingly and allows me to place the handcuffs on his wrists without so much as a sound. I could not get myself to believe that he was capable of murder, but there are a lot of things in this case that have exceeded my understanding. My duty was to arrest him; it is up to the judge and jury to decide his guilt.

~~~~~~~

I hear music as my mounted guards and I approach the Pine Level jail with the prisoners who are connected to the second murder. It's not particularly nice music, but it's clearly an attempt.

As usual the warden meets me as I approach with the wagon. He quickly instructs his guards to take the three new prisoners to their cells.
~~~~~~~

"What's that sound?" I ask.

"I guess you could call it music." He chuckles. "The church congregation wanted to provide some things for the prisoners to pass the time. They seem to enjoy using the instruments to try to create songs together. And their family members have been here often. They bring all kinds of things. Did you know that Willard is an excellent artist?"

I am stunned. "No, I can honestly say I had no idea." I am slightly surprised by the jovial mood surrounding the jail, but as long as the prisoners are still here for their trial, I will let the warden run this place as he sees fit.

It's not as cold as it had been when we were here a couple of weeks ago, but we still accept the kindness of the pastor to sleep in the church rather than outside. We enter the church, and each select our own pew as our space for evening. I purposefully take a spot away from the others, and they understand my cue that I don't want to talk tonight. I fall asleep to the sound of their hushed conversation.

Chapter Twelve

"You are not going to believe this," Alden states as he walks into my home without knocking. He's swinging around a rolled-up newspaper as he speaks. We have become much closer over this ordeal, but he still usually uses proper manners.

"What's happening, Alden?"

He slams the newspaper on to my table and unrolls it. "Look here, front page of the *New York Times*. Adelaide's sister mailed this to us." Alden places his finger on an article.

I lean over the table and read the headline: "An Assassination Society. The Bloody Work of a Band of Southern Murders."

"What the hell?" My mind spins; I grab the paper with both hands and slump down in the chair to read it. Fannie ushers all the little children outside. Clem sits at the chair directly across the table from me.

"What is it, Pa?" Clem asks.

I am too engrossed in the article to answer immediately. Clem taps the table as he anxiously waits for me to finish.

"Well?" Alden says.

"How did they get this information? It's not even all correct."

Clem takes the paper from my hands and begins to read it himself.

"It's a good story and newspaper men love a good story. Especially, adding the scandal of the strong reputation of Bidwell's family up north."

"But they are printing hearsay. How far do you think this story has spread?"

"Well, if they printed in the *New York Times*, it's likely getting printed in other papers around the country as well."

I shake my head in disbelief; I did not expect this to be a sensation outside of our area.

Clem looks up as he finishes the story, "Well, at least they got one thing right."

"What's that?" I ask.

"They are an assassination society. That's much more accurate than the name that they gave themselves." Alden and I nod in agreement. Alden finally takes a seat at the table with Clem and me.

"I apologize for my brash entrance. I think I was just shocked that this was in the *New York Times*, on the front page to boot. But I guess, what's done is done, and we can't waste our time on things that we cannot control."

"You are right, Alden. I am sure this will blow over and the newspapers will go back to ignoring us."

"Excuse me, Major Adams," a shy Fannie chimes in from the doorway.

"Yes, sweetheart?" He smiles at her.

"We have been learning about France in school, and I think it sounds like a wonderful place, and I was wondering if you could tell me a little more about it."

Alden's broad grin covers his entire face. "Ce serait avec plaisir."

Fannie's eyes light up. "Was that French? It's beautiful!"

~~~~~~~

Spring in Florida is incredible. It's hard to explain to northerners, who are used to spring unfolding out of the bare trees and empty landscape. We don't have the bleakness of winter, but the blooms that come in the spring are so spectacular that you don't need that juxtaposition. The children are all out in the yard playing on this beautiful April day when Furman Whitaker rides up. He dismounts his horse and ties it to my hitching post out front.

"Good morning, Sheriff." He tips his hat as he approaches.

"Well, Furman. What a pleasant surprise. What brings you to these parts?"
~~~~~~~

"I was paying some visits and thought I would stop in to see your family and check in on the status of the trial."

"Well, I'm mighty pleased that you did. Would you like some lemonade?"

"That would be nice, thank you."

I offer him a seat in a chair on the front porch and go into the house to fetch the pitcher and a couple of glasses. When I return, Fannie is already on the porch asking Furman about his son Harper.

"Actually, that was something I wanted to share with you all. Nellie is with child again and we hope to have another baby this summer."

"That's wonderful news," Fannie exclaims. "Maybe if you are lucky, you will have a family as large as ours someday."

As if on cue, Wade and Will begin arguing loudly inside the house.

"Boys!" I bellow. The arguing stops. "Yes," I say with a smile, "if you are lucky."

Furman laughs in return and accepts the glass of lemonade that I hand him. I pour myself a glass and sit in the chair next to him.

"It was nice talking with you, Mr. Whitaker," Fannie says kindly, and then makes the proper exit to allow the adults to speak.

"If all my children are half as wonderful as her, I will be very pleased," Furman says with a smile.

"Thank you, she is truly a gift. How have things been going with the family?"

"Honestly, Sheriff, I am surprised by people and their continued desire to take care of the murders on their own. There have been times when people are downright threatening to us because we want this to be a lawful trial."

"I am sorry to hear that. Do you and your family feel safe?"

"Most of the time."

"Is there anything I can do to help?"

"I don't think so, but I appreciate all of your work so far. We are lucky to have you as our sheriff."

My mind begins to ruminate again on the fact that I could have stopped Charles's murder if I had just investigated Riley's. But then I look at Furman. And I remember that he was one of the people on the list of people to kill, and I am thankful that those murderers will not get the chance to take his life too.

"How's Charlotte? Has she been able to mourn?"

"We actually just returned from a trip to Illinois. Charlotte had a monument placed in the cemetery up there.

We had a nice memorial ceremony, and Carrie was able to join us from her school in Chicago."

"That sounds lovely. Once again, I am deeply sorry that we are not able to recover his body."

"Sheriff, that is not yours to apologize for; you did your best. The apology should come from those bastards that dumped him there." We both know in our hearts that that is never going to happen.

"But Charlotte had the last word," Furman continues, "the monument read that he was assassinated in Sarasota, Florida."

"Really? She had that engraved on the stone?"

"She sure did. Along with a verse from Revelation that says, 'And the sea shall give up its dead.'"

"Good for her! She is a brave and noble woman, and I am constantly impressed by her."

"I don't know if she will stay in the area after the trial. Too much sorrow, anger, and fear."

"I can't say I blame her."

"Do you know when the trial will occur?"

"Honestly, I am surprised that it is taking this long. I am not sure what the holdup is with the Circuit Court. But it better be soon—our county jail is at capacity!"

Chapter Thirteen

It rains in Florida during the summer. More accurately, it rains a lot in Florida during the summer. It rains so much that my men and I are currently riding our horses through water that is now over the tops of our boots. We are headed out to Pine Level for the much-anticipated trials for the murders of Harrison "Tip" Riley and Charles Abbe. No thanks to the newspapers for spreading the story far and wide, the judge had quite a time finding an impartial jury. Plus, the family and supporters of the prisoners have been spreading a great deal of propaganda. They went so far as to have pamphlets printed and distributed trying to twist the story to make the victims the villains. I know that they are trying to protect their families, but to fabricate such lies . . . I tried to stop it at first, but as much as I have lost my respect for them, I still hold the U.S. Constitution in high esteem, so I must give them their free speech.

As we approach Pine Level, I can see the courthouse from quite a distance over the flat barren land. But my eyes are tired from squinting into the sun, and the humidity makes the air heavy and difficult to see through clearly. Even with all of that, it seems that a large crowd has gathered.

"Do you see that?" I ask George.

He raises a hand to block the bright sun from his eyes. "It looks like we are going to have a packed house for the trial.

I suppose that everyone from Braidentown to Sarasota has come to watch."

But as we get closer, I do not recognize any of the faces. Someone in the crowd yells, "That's the sheriff!" And people begin to come forward to meet us. Everyone is talking over one other. I hear bits and pieces, but I am not able to differentiate who is saying what.

"Sheriff Watson, I'm a with the *Florida Times-Union*."

"Sheriff, did Bidwell really attempt suicide?"

"*Orange County Reporter*, here."

"Is it true that you allowed them to murder Mr. Riley in cold blood?"

"*South Georgia Times*, I have a few questions."

My mind races. Why have these people traveled so far for our trial? How do they know so much about this? What should I say to them?

"The sheriff will not be answering any questions." Major Adams's voice rises over all the chaos, and there is a very brief lull in the noise before the members of the press begin chattering again. George and I carefully dismount our horses while Alden forces his way through the crowd to my side.

"Do not talk to any of them, do you understand?" George and I both nod. There is no need to attempt to respond otherwise; we would not be heard over the din.

The trial is set to begin tomorrow. I believe we will be able to sleep in the church as usual, but I have no idea where all these people are going to go. The courthouse will probably seat around 200. In my wildest dreams, I never thought that wouldn't be enough space. Muddy horses and wagons are scattered all around the jail and courthouse. I knew this had been big news when it happened, but that was months ago. I didn't think it was still of interest, and I definitely didn't expect the reporters to travel so far in the hot, wet summer to the middle of nowhere.

I see the pastor in the crowd. He is carrying around a basket with a container of water to fill people's canteens.

"Well, Sheriff, Pine Level has never seen the likes of this."

"And hopefully, it never will again," I reply as he pours some water into my canteen.

"I want to offer the church again. This time to you, the judges, and the victims' families. We have arranged for the families of the accused to stay in the courthouse."

"That is mighty kind of you." I appreciate his thoughtfulness in separating the two groups but treating them both with compassion.

The warden approaches and we exchange the proper pleasantries even though they seem trite among the chaos.

"Sheriff," he begins, "we have all local guards on duty and have added a few more for the days of the trials. In addition to guarding the jail, they will also be guarding the church and courthouse." He lifts his hat and wipes some sweat from his brow with the back of his hand.

"That was smart thinking. Thank you." The sun is setting now, and I hope that it will bring some relief from the heat. But the setting sun also means that the bugs will soon be emerging for the evening.

I thank both the pastor and the warden before making my way through the crowd to the church. Among the crowd of people, I occasionally spot a familiar face and nod to them as I pass. Inside the church, I find Alden with three men who I do not recognize.

"Ahhh, there he is!" Alden says as I enter. "Sheriff, it is my pleasure to introduce you to Judge Mitchell, Mr. Stephen Sparkman the attorney, and Mr. Bob Griffith the scribe."

I shake each man's hand and stop at Mr. Griffith. "The man with the most difficult job of the trial."

Bob smiles, "Don't worry, Sheriff, I have brought more paper and ink than I have ever used in a trial."

The doors open and we see the pastor enter with his arm around Charlotte. Charlotte is now in full mourning attire; I assume she was able to obtain the proper pieces when they were in Illinois for the memorial service. Behind her is Furman with Nellie, heavy with child, on his arm. Bless her, we are all sweltering in this heat, but she looks miserable. I am surprised that she made the trip in her condition, but that shows that she inherited the fortitude of her mother. They take a seat in a pew near the back of the church.

Tomorrow morning, Charlotte and I will both have to take the stand. I am not looking forward to having to relive the murder scene again, but I can't fathom how much she must be dreading this herself.

I approach the family. They each nod a polite hello.

"Charlotte, is there anything I can do for you?"

"Thank you, Sheriff. You have done so much already. We truly can't thank you enough."

I appreciate her words, but I doubt that I will ever feel as if I have done enough for them.

"We will let you know if there is anything, Sheriff," Furman replies.

At this time, many people are eating the food they brought with them. I watch as Nellie is unsuccessful in getting her mother to take a biscuit. Over the mutter in the room, I hear her plead, "Mother, you need your energy."

I move towards the front of the church and sit in the pew next to Alden. He offers me a peach. "It's from my own garden," he says with pride. I take it and thank him. I thank him again after I take a bite and realize how delicious it is.

Within a couple of hours, everyone has made a spot to sleep. Some have bed tack that they placed on the floor, and some are curled up in pews with their jackets balled up as pillows. But no one has a blanket on; it is way too hot for that.

I listen to some quiet murmurs as I drift off to sleep. Once again, I have no idea what to expect tomorrow.

Chapter Fourteen

I awake to odd sounds, and it takes me a couple of moments to remember where I am. The peculiar sound that I hear is the tin of Alden's pail as he pulls out a couple more peaches and some biscuits for breakfast. I stretch as I stand up and slowly roll my head around to get the kinks out. I appreciate sleeping in the church, but I am already missing my bed and I don't know how long this is going to last. Some kind members of the congregation have brought water and bowls for us to wash up. I welcome the cool splash to my face. Everyone is awake at this point, and I move away from the water basin to allow the next person to use it.

I use my wet hands to try to smooth my hair and beard into place and then secure my tie around my neck. I don't have a mirror to check my appearance, but with this heat, I think we are all going to look a mess anyway. I don't bother grabbing my hat since I will just have to take it off in the courthouse. My mind is going over the schedule and tasks for the day, and I walk out of the church consumed in my thoughts.

I am startled back to reality when I open the door. The morning sun is bright on the horizon, steam is rising from the ground, hitting any bystander directly in the face while the reporters are standing at attention with their notebooks and pencils ready.

I walk down the front steps and try not to make eye contact with any reporters. I am getting better at ignoring their chatter as I make the short trip to the courthouse without any incidents. Two guards are stationed at the entrance of the courthouse to keep out the reporters; I nod at them as I enter the nearly empty building. Two more guards are silently standing near the back of the courtroom, and I hear people in one of the small back rooms. The courthouse is small and consists of the main courtroom with two smaller rooms in the back for the judge and the jury deliberation. I head to the room to the right where I hear the noise and see Judge Mitchell, a couple of the state attorneys, the warden, and the bailiff.

"Good morning," I greet them all as I enter. We exchange pleasantries. Major Adams arrives shortly after I do.

"Now that we are all here," the judge says, "let's review the order of today's trial." I notice that he looks a little pale. It must be mighty hot in that robe. The judge goes over the day and then instructs the bailiff to have the guards open the doors.

"Are you ready for this?" Alden looks at me as we walk through the door back into the courtroom.

I survey the swarm of people entering the double doors from the outside. "Honestly, I just can't wait for this to be over." The courthouse is a sad building to begin with but adding the heat and the large crowd has made it downright pathetic. We take our seats on a long wooden bench. The windows are open, but I don't know if the slight breeze is worth all the bugs. It's still early in the morning, but I don't see a single face that's not moist with sweat. Many people are frantically waving hand fans as they scramble to find a seat. Within moments, all the benches are packed, and people are lining the sides and back of the room as well. The doors are still open, and I can see that there are still many people attempting to listen from outside.

"All rise!" the bailiff instructs. He waits for the crowd to stand and quiet. "The honorable Judge Mitchell presiding." The judge enters from the back room and takes his seat at the bench; well, it is at the table that is being used as a bench.

"Please be seated," he says. I am impressed with how quiet the crowd has become. They all want to hear every word. I nod at Bob as he poises his pen to begin the task of documenting every word uttered during the trial.

Charles Moorehouse is the first witness called to the stand. Once again, he retells the events of that fateful day. I feel sorry for this innocent young man getting wrapped up in this whole ordeal. He just happened to be at the wrong place at the wrong time. The fact that the murderers were willing to commit this crime with an eyewitness is a stark reminder of how little they respect the local law. I turn slightly to my left to see the prisoners out of the corner of my eye. I wonder what they think of the local law now. I smirk a bit at that thought.

The next witness is Charlotte Abbe. She rises as she is called to the stand. If possible, the room falls even more silent than before. Her footsteps are tiny, but powerful. Her long, black tulle veil sways gently behind her. As she takes her oath, she looks straight ahead, never once allowing her glance to fall upon the thugs that murdered her husband. I don't turn around to look, but I would bet that her eyes are locked on her daughter Nellie. Charlotte sits with her back perfectly straight. Her voice cracks a couple of times while she gives her testimony, but she never fully breaks down. When she is finished, she stands, walks confidently down the center aisle, and straight out the door. Nellie and Furman stand and follow her as she passes by their bench. Several reporters leave the room too. I hope the reporters are leaving for fresh air and not to pester the family, but I assume it is the latter.

"Sheriff Alexander Watson is called to the stand."

I am next. I have recounted this so many times since the murder, in conversation, in testimony, and in my mind. So, I was surprised by the nerves that overtake me when I stand. Maybe it's just the heat. I feel slightly shaky as I make my way to front of the room and have a new appreciation for how steadily Charlotte was able to make that walk.

I turn to face the crowd. I place my right hand on the Bible. A bead of sweat rolls down my spine, and I hear a gnat buzzing in my right ear as I repeat the oath. What has come over me? Why am I suddenly so nervous? But then I take a hard look at the murderers. Only Willard, Anderson, and Bacon are on trial today. I take a good look at each. Willard is dressed nicely with a white shirt and narrow tie. He looks much healthier now than when we first brought him in. He looks back at me, but then quickly looks away. Anderson is also cleaned up for the trial. He is sweating more than the others and is looking down at the floor. Ed Bacon's hair is shaved short now; he catches my eye and grins. That's all I needed. The nerves are gone. Let's convict these bastards.

The first day concludes with George Riggin's testimony and then we file out of the courthouse. It is still hot outside, but I can breathe. I pull at my collar a bit for some air and inhale deeply.

~~~~~~~

The next morning, we leave the church a little early and take all our belongings so that they can hold Sunday services. I would estimate over half of the members of the press left at the end of day yesterday. I suppose they are going to try to get back to their offices and get the first day of the trial in print. There is no way to predict exactly how long this will take, but I anticipate another day or so. For now, we have one day of rest.

The trial begins again on Monday morning. With all the reporters who left, everyone has a seat in the courtroom today but just barely. As we listen to the testimonies, I hear the soft melody of raindrops on the roof. It rains at least once each day, usually around four or five in the afternoon. You can almost tell time by the summer storms.

The trial continues somewhat uneventfully until midday on Wednesday. After the final arguments are heard, the jury enters the back room behind the judge on the left and the door shuts loudly behind them. Slowly, everyone in the courtroom stands and leaves the building to get some air. Many of the reporters have returned by this time; they must have simply gone back as fast as they could to write the story and then came back just as quickly.
~~~~~~~

Alden and I stand outside together. We have spent every moment together for the past five days, so we don't have much to say to each other anymore. The day's rain has not yet come, so the air is thick, hot, and sticky. I hear the sound of an untuned guitar and wonder which of the prisoners is playing.

I turn toward the jail and see Alfred Bidwell wife's exiting. She is sobbing loudly as someone helps her down the ladder. Bidwell is not on trial for the death of Abbe, but he will be in a couple of days for the murder of Tip. His family is convinced that he will be pardoned. As difficult as it has been for me to accept that these men are capable of such horrors, I can't imagine how the families are able to handle this. But facts are facts. No matter how they attempt to spin their motives, the facts have been presented repeatedly over these past few days. Maybe these men didn't start with the intention of murder, but that is where it ended and they all played a part, some more than others. It is easy to place all the blame on Willard because he pulled the trigger, but one must never underestimate the influence of a group or a mob.

I enter the church to get a little something to eat and drink. Thank goodness for the kindness of the congregation; I will have to remember to pack more food for the next trial. After my quick snack, I decide to take a little walk. There really is nothing to see in Pine Level. I notice a large black storm cloud rolling in from the west and hear a small clap of thunder in the distance. Immediately after the thunder I hear Alden calling from down the road.

"Sandy, they have reached a verdict."

I quicken my pace and enter the courthouse just before I hear the first raindrops on the roof. The storm is perfectly timed today. I sit down in my usual spot next to Alden and wait. It is only a few more moments before the door to the jury room opens, but by this time, the rain is falling so hard it is difficult to hear. The reporters surround the courthouse and lean inside the windows in hopes of hearing.

Judge Mitchell walks out and takes his seat; he has not fared well over the past few days. His color has become more and more pale, and there are now dark circles around his eyes. A juror, holding a piece of paper, walks to the front of the judge. The other jurors follow behind him and line up in front of their chairs. The one juror stands at an angle to address both the judge and the room.

"We, the jury, find Charles B. Willard and Joseph C. Anderson guilty of murder in the first degree. We beg the mercy of the court." He pauses as the room erupts in gasps and cries.

"Order, order!" The judge hammers his gavel but is obviously struggling to do so. The room quiets again.

"We, the jury, find Edmund C. Bacon not guilty." The room erupts again.

"Order! Order!" The judge tries in vain this time to calm the room. The guards surround the guilty men. Willard and Anderson are silent and pale. Bacon is laughing. I am disappointed that he was not found guilty, but I agree that the jury came to the correct verdict based on the evidence presented in this case. But he's not in the clear yet, he will be on trial again soon for Riley's murder.

I notice the bailiff holding the judge's arm as he leads him to the back room. I follow.

"Is everything ok?" The rain has slowed down now, but the ruckus in the courthouse still makes it difficult to hear.

"Sheriff," Judge Mitchell struggles to speak. "I will deliver my verdict in a day or so, but we are going to have to call a new judge for the next trial. I apologize if this causes a delay, but I am not well."

"Of course," I respond, "is there anything I can do to help?"

"No, no. Simply keep doing what you are doing."

I look back out into the courtroom. Bacon is still smiling as the guard leads him out of the building.

~~~~~~~

My hope that the sentence would be decided the next day fades with the sun. We sent a messenger in the morning to request another judge for the Riley trial, but other than that we sit around under whatever shade we can find. This has been a long week, and I am anxious to get a little time at home with my family before I must return for the second trial. A large number of the reporters remain. I guess the real story is in the sentence not the verdict. Ignoring them has become second nature to me now.
~~~~~~~

I head to the courthouse first thing Friday morning; Judge Mitchell is already in the back room with a couple of other people. He is fanning himself with a hand fan. It is hot, and we are all sweating, but the beads of sweat on his forehead are not from the weather. I decide not to get close enough to shake his hand today. The judge can be replaced for a trial, but the sheriff at the scene cannot.

"I have made a decision, Sheriff," he says faintly as I enter. "I have sent for the defendants to be brought over. Please share the word and gather . . ." he stops short and swallows hard.

"I will take care of it, your Honor. You save your energy for the trip home."

I leave the courthouse and tell the first few people I see that the judge is about to give the sentence. I watch as word spreads across the people scattered throughout the landscape. They begin making their way over, and the courthouse is quickly full again. Reporters have their pencils poised in the ready position as the judge takes the stand one final time.

"Charles Willard and Joseph Anderson, you have been found guilty by a jury of your peers of murder in the first degree of Charles Abbe. I hereby sentence you to life imprisonment."

Gasps and chatter again fill the courtroom. Alden and I make our way out through the crowd so that we can talk.

"Well," he begins, "what do you think?"

"I think justice was served."

“So do I.”

Chapter Fifteen

I hold little Cliff propped on my hip and gaze out over the river. Clem stands next to me while the young children are playing. He knows that I need this solitude, but he also has a lot of questions about the trial and can't help himself from asking them. He has become a very smart young man and, normally, I would happily answer all his questions, but I need a break from talking about this trial. I decide to change the subject.

"Any young ladies who you fancy?"

"What?" He is taken aback by the abrupt topic switch. He blushes.

"I will take that as a yes." Clem turned sixteen this past February, I am sure he has been looking.

"Mary is really sweet," he replies sheepishly.

I am about to ask more when we are interrupted by Wade and Will with little Eva and Alex desperately trying to keep up with them. Fannie is following behind them with her arms full of sticks and shells.

"Look at all of the treasures we found!" Will is so excited he is barely able to get the words out.

“We are going to take them home and start a treasure chest,” Wade adds.

“Pa, maybe you could bring us something from Pine Level for the treasure chest.” Will beams with his new idea.

“Well, there’s not much out there, but I will see what I can find.” I laugh at the thought of what kind of treasure could possibly be in Pine Level.

“It looks like there is a storm rolling in,” Clem says as he looks at a dark cloud in the distance.

“Let’s back up, kids.” I place Cliff back in the pram and Fannie loads all the twins’ treasures around him. When her arms are empty, she wipes off the sand and dirt.

“If you two are going to be treasure hunters,” she says to the twins, “then you are going to have to learn to carry them yourself.”

I laugh as we make our way back to the house.

~~~~~~~

Tuesday morning, I mount my horse to once more head out to Pine Level. Alden left yesterday so that he could get there early to meet the new judge who was replacing Judge Mitchell. The sun will be visible over the horizon soon; it is that time of day when the soft light is just beginning to make shapes clear. I had said goodbye to the children before they went to bed last night. I want this trial to be conducted properly, but I also want it done be quickly. Not only do I
~~~~~~~

want to put this whole ordeal behind me, but also I want to be home. Fannie and Clem have been incredible throughout all of this, but it isn't fair to them.

The journey has become familiar, but this is the first time in a long while that I take it on my own. I appreciate the rest from talking and listening. I had hoped that it would also be a break from thinking, but that must be too much to ask. It's great to have the extended light of these long summer days. The heat hasn't let up at all, neither has the rain. I hit a few areas of water along the way, but nothing as deep as during our travel for the first trial.

I don't know why I am still surprised by the number of reporters outside the jail when I arrive at Pine Level. I guess I assumed that they were most interested in the Abbe case, but it appears that the story is now about the members of the Vigilance Committee and not about who they killed.

I had been blocking them out, but I decide to listen in on their conversation today as I walk through the crowd and head to the courthouse. I catch part of a conversation about Bidwell; they don't believe he will be convicted due to his family's power up north. Another man is talking about his belief that the leaders are the only ones who should be tried since those performing the murders were under duress. And just before I walk into the courthouse, I hear another person mention that the sheriff is to blame and is unfit for the position. I wonder if they intended for me to hear that. Regardless, this comment reminds me why I usually ignore them all. I nod at the guards, enter the building, and head directly to the back room on the right.

"Here he is," Alden greets me with a renewed energy. I think we both needed that short break. "Sheriff Watson, I would like to introduce you to Judge Foster."

"Thank you for filling in like this," I say as I shake his hand.

"I was just telling Major Adams how impressed I am with the work that you have done. Uncovering this group and bringing them justice was a monumental task, and the fact that you two did it with such limited resources is astounding."

"Thank you," I respond in earnest. I didn't realize how much I was letting the chatter of the reporters affect me, but it had been and I appreciate this compliment even more now.

It's getting late, and we all head to our usual spots in the church for the night.

~~~~~~~

The next morning, Alden and I make our way back into the courthouse to take our seats. I watch as the prisoners are led into the room. Bidwell, Cato, and Hunter are groomed and well-dressed. Dr. Andrews is also well-dressed, but he looks unwell. I wonder if he is suffering from the same ailment that afflicted Judge Mitchell. Bacon is his usual egotistical self, but what truly surprises me is Tom Dryman. Gone was the quiet man who wouldn't make eye contact at his home and in his place is an Ed Bacon imitator. He follows closely behind Bacon and mimics his walk. Bacon occasionally turns and says something, undoubtedly crass, to Dryman, who responds with a hearty laugh. Bacon has his
~~~~~~~

audience, and Dryman has a friend. It is easy to see now how Tom was manipulated into being part of this group. I avert my gaze from the two of them and bow my head in a quick prayer before the trial begins.

Abbe's trial was focused on the actual murder, but the trial for Harrison "Tip" Riley has become the trial of the Sarasota Vigilance Committee. Six men are on trial today, several of whom are considered upstanding men of means. Well, they were considered that.

"All rise for the Honorable Judge Foster." The room rises and Judge Foster enters to begin the trial.

Immediately a motion to sever Cato and Dryman from the trial is made. Although it isn't stated why publicly, we all know that it is because those two are willing to provide additional information and need to be protected. Judge Foster grants the motion, and the two men are escorted from the room.

Judge Foster moves the trial along much more quickly than Judge Mitchell did, and the closing arguments conclude midday on Friday. We break while the jury deliberates, and I decide to take a walk. I walk quickly through the press. I've learned that eavesdropping on their conversations does me no good, so I don't pay attention, finding my way to a tree near the church. I sit on the ground and lean against the strong trunk of the oak. I take a long drink from my canteen, and as I am securing the cap, I notice an interesting feather. As if on cue, the owl hoots above me. So much for being nocturnal, I think, as I look up to see if I can spy him in the tree. His small white face is only a few branches above me, and it is clear that this is one of his feathers.

"If you don't mind," I say to the owl, "I would like to take this home to my sons for their treasure box." The owl cocks its head, and I take that as a yes.

The jury reaches their verdict quickly, and we all file back into the hot and steamy courtroom. The judge comes out of his chambers, and the jury is called forward. A young man who could not have been more than twenty years old steps forward with the verdict in his hand.

"We, the jury, find Leonard F. Andrews and Alfred B. Bidwell guilty of accessory before the fact of murder in the first degree."

A sorrowful cry rises above the chatter in the room, and Mrs. Bidwell falls to her knees in hysterics. A couple of people help her to her feet and escort her outside before the juror continues.

"We find Edmund P. Bacon guilty of principle in murder of the first degree." The crowd begins to murmur again, but Bacon doesn't show any sort of emotion.

"And the jury finds Adam W. Hunter not guilty. So, say we all."

This time, the jury did not recommend mercy.

~~~~~~~
~~~~~~~

Judge Foster decides on the sentence overnight, and we all gather again early on Saturday morning to hear. The silence is palpable as the judge takes his bench.

"I hereby sentence Leonard F. Andrews, Alfred B. Bidwell, and Edmund P. Bacon to death for the murder of Harrison T. Riley."

The room erupts in pure commotion; I stand ready in case any of the guards need assistance. Mrs. Bidwell is screaming, "He's innocent!" over and over at the top of her lungs. Alfred Bidwell is very pale and obviously in a state of shock. Dr. Andrews looks ill. Once again, Bacon doesn't flinch.

Since the verdict was given early in the day, I decide to head home. I was in familiar territory by the time night fell and was able to sneak into the house. I was rather exhausted and slept in a little later than usual on Sunday morning. Fannie and Clem are already in the kitchen when I awake.

"Pa!" they exclaim in unison as I descended the stairs.

"I saw your boots this morning, so I knew you were here, but I didn't want to wake you. You must be so exhausted, but I do have a lot of questions," Fannie was talking quickly, and I knew that I needed to sit down and talk to her about all that has occurred over the last seven months.

"I will tell you everything after church services," I promise, as she tightly wraps her arms around me and buries her face into my chest.

"I'm just so happy that this is over," she whispers.

"Me too, sweetheart." I truly hope it is over.

John and Elizabeth Curry greet us at the wagon and help get all the children down.

"It is good to see you again," John says as he claps me on the shoulder.

"I am sure everyone is curious to hear about the trial," I respond.

"Yes," says Elizabeth, "but we are even more happy to have you home safe and sound." I smile back at her and thank her for her kind words as we all enter the church.

As I sit in the center of the pew with Cliff in my lap and the twins placed strategically far apart on each end as usual, I begin to give thanks for all the wonderful people I have met since moving to Florida. Settling here was a risk and there have been hard times. But as I look at the people in the church, I see all the reasons why it was worth it.

Epilogue

Fannie Watson
December 25, 1890

"Hi, Ma," I say as I look down at the familiar tombstone in front of me, "Merry Christmas!"

It is chilly today, so I wrap my shawl tighter around my shoulders as my long skirt moves slightly in the breeze. At the base of the stone, I see a wilting sprig of beautyberry and I know that Pa was here yesterday.

"Oh Ma, as usual, Will and Wade were up before sunrise waiting to see what was in their stockings. They are fourteen years old now. Sometimes they act like young gentlemen, and sometimes they are still children." I pause for a moment and look up at the Spanish moss swinging above me in the large oak tree. "You know, Pa still hangs your stocking on the mantle." Tears begin to roll down my face in warm streaks.

"We had an unexpected visitor this morning before we left for church. It was Mr. Johnson, the postmaster. He had a telegram to show Pa. Alfred Bidwell, you know, one of the leaders of that assassination group. He was pardoned today."

"Pa rarely talks about the murders, but I could see that he was upset by the news of Bidwell's release. He worked so hard to ensure that justice was served, and now most have escaped or have been pardoned. I think only two are still in prison, but now they let the leader go. I think they will all be released soon too."

"Sometimes, Ma," I sigh deeply, "sometimes I am so scared that those men are going to come after Pa."

"But Pa has taught me to focus on the good people in the world. And there are so many good people! I visit Major Adams and Adelaide often now. They are teaching me about other countries, and I have even learned a little French. I truly want to go to France someday. Do you think that's possible, Ma?"

I pause and stand in silence for a bit imagining what it would be like to travel to another country. The sun peeks out from behind a cloud above me and casts a light on Ma's grave.

"I've been meaning to ask you, Ma. Have you met Pliny Reason up in Heaven yet? Pa and I both became real fond of him, and it was devastating when the yellow fever killed him. But I know that he is in Heaven with you now, and I am sure you will like him." I smile at the thought of the two of them looking down on me.

"Everyone is doing well here; I think you would be proud of us all. Clem is still at home. Sometimes I think I am going to get married before he does! The twins will never change; I love that they are such energetic, curious people. And the little ones are getting so big now. Alex and Eva are doing great in school, and little Cliff loves to be outdoors. He's always up in a tree somewhere."

"Oh, Ma! Mrs. Curry taught me to make an apple cake! I am going to surprise everyone at dinner tonight. They are going to love it."

"I know you would love it too. I miss you so much." I drop to my knees, put my head on the ground, and cry.

After a few moments, I take a deep breath and slowly stand up. I brush the grass off my skirt and straighten my bonnet. I try never to break down like that, but today, with the holidays and learning about Bidwell's release, I guess it was just too much. But the family needs me to be strong. It is Christmas after all.

"I love you, Ma. Forever." I say aloud. I turn and walk slowly toward the road.

Author's Note

The story of the Sarasota (Sara Sota) Vigilance Committee (or the Sarasota Assassination Society) has continued to intrigue people in the Sarasota and Bradenton areas. Many versions of the story have been told, and a mythos has formed around the tale.

Why is this story still so captivating? I do not believe that it is simply due to a fascination with true crime and mystery. I think it is much deeper. It is a tale that we see repeated too often in our society. People create an other and are convinced that this created other is a threat.

As I researched the story, many of the characters came to life for me. I was surprised by my connection to Fannie. She was not the easiest one to get to know. I started out with only the initials F. A., but she was slowly revealed to me and now has a special place in my heart. Unfortunately, I learned the most about her from her obituary. Fannie gave birth to her first child on September 17, 1897, passing away the next day at the age of twenty-three.

I also want to thank Bob Griffith, the court stenographer. The speed at which he wrote to record the trials often made it difficult to read, but even that urgency in writing told part of the story.

And dear, Pliny Reasoner. His letters home gave insight into the feelings of the community. This is not something that

I could have discovered in court documents. I am grateful for his eloquence and lovely penmanship and to the Florida Agricultural Archives for preserving these documents. Pliny made a name for himself in the world of agriculture by the age of twenty-five. He passed away from yellow fever in 1888.

And last, but certainly not least, I would like to thank my mother for fostering my love of history and buying me the American Girl books which ignited my love of historical fiction.

Made in United States
Orlando, FL
18 July 2023

35247154R00085